Grade 4

INTERACTIVE
Read-Aloud
ANTHOLOGY WITH PLAYS

Macmillan/McGraw-Hill

ACKNOWLEDGMENTS

"The Case of the Muscle Maker" from ENCYCLOPEDIA BROWN SOLVES THEM ALL by Donald J. Sobol. Copyright © 1968 by Donald J. Sobol. Used by permission of Thomas Nelson Inc.

"Some Rivers" by Frank Asch from MY AMERICA: A POETRY ATLAS OF THE UNITED STATES by Lee Bennett Hopkins. Copyright © 2000 by Lee Bennett Hopkins. Used by permission of Simon & Schuster Books for Young Readers, an imprint of Simon & Schuster Children's Publishing Division.

"Persistence" by Paul W. Richards from *Highlights for Children*, January 2004, Vol. 59, Issue 1. Copyright © 2004 by Highlights for Children. Used by permission of Highlights for Children.

Excerpt from WILD AND SWAMPY by Jim Arnosky. Copyright © 2000 by Jim Arnosky. Used by permission of HarperCollins Publishers.

Excerpt from LILY AND MISS LIBERTY by Carla Stevens. Copyright © 1992 by Carla Stevens. Used by permission of Scholastic Inc.

"Erh-Lang and the Suns" from THE MAGIC BOAT AND OTHER CHINESE FOLK STORIES by M. A. Jagendorf and Virginia Weng. Copyright © 1980 by M. A. Jagendorf and Virginia Weng. Used by permission of Gage Publishing Co.

"What REA Service Means to Our Farm Home" by Rose Dudley Scearce from *Rural Electrification News*, March 1939. Copyright © 1939 by Rural Electrification Administration. Used by permission of Rural Electrification Administration.

"The Odd Couple," "Yes, Deer," and "Spotty Friendship" from *National Geographic Kids*, May, July/August, and September 2004. Copyright © 2004 by National Geographic Kids. Used by permission of National Geographic Kids.

"I Have a Dream," excerpt from speech by Dr. Martin Luther King, Jr. Copyright © 1963 by Writers House. Used by permission of Writers House.

Excerpt from THE GET RICH QUICK CLUB by Dan Gutman. Copyright © 2004 by Dan Gutman. Used by permission of HarperCollins Publishers.

"Old Crow Warriors" by Frederick M. Howe III, from NIGHT IS GONE, DAY IS STILL COMING, edited by Annette Piña Ochoa, Betsy Franco, and Traci L. Gourdine. Copyright © 2003 by Annette Piña Ochoa, Betsy Franco, and Traci L. Gourdine. Used by permission of Candlewick Press.

WATER DANCE by Thomas Locker. Copyright © 1997 by Thomas Locker. Used by permission of Harcourt Brace & Company.

HACHIKO: THE TRUE STORY OF A LOYAL DOG by Pamela S. Turner. Copyright © 2004 by Pamela S. Turner. Used by permission of Houghton Mifflin Company.

"At the Flick of a Switch" from EARTH LINES: POEMS FOR THE GREEN AGE by Pat Moon. Copyright © 1991 by Pat Moon. Used by permission of Greenwillow Books/HarperCollins Publishers.

WHALE IN THE SKY by Anne Siberell. Copyright © 1982 by Anne Siberell. Used by permission of E.P. Dutton, Inc.

Continued on page 234

B

The McGraw·Hill Companies

 Macmillan/McGraw-Hill

Published by Macmillan/McGraw-Hill, of McGraw-Hill Education, a division of The McGraw-Hill Companies, Inc., Two Penn Plaza, New York, New York 10121.

Printed in the United States of America

6 7 8 9 10 HSO 14 13 12 11 10

CONTENTS

Plays and Choral Readings

Think-Aloud Copying Masters

INTERACTIVE
Read-Aloud
ANTHOLOGY with PLAYS

Developing Listening Comprehension

Read Alouds help to build students' listening comprehension. This anthology offers selections from a variety of genres, including biography, fiction, folktales, nonfiction, primary sources, songs, and poetry, to share with students. Instruction is provided with each selection to develop specific **comprehension strategies.** Students are asked to **set a purpose for listening** as well as to **determine the author's purpose** for writing. Using the instruction provided, each Read Aloud becomes an enjoyable, purposeful learning experience.

What Makes a Read Aloud Interactive?

With each selection, **Teacher Think Alouds** are provided to help you model the use of comprehension strategies during reading. Using Think Alouds allows students to listen and to observe how a good reader uses strategies to get meaning from text. After reading, students are given the opportunity to apply the comprehension strategy. Students are asked to "think aloud" as they apply the strategy. By listening to a **Student Think Aloud** you can determine if the student is applying the comprehension strategy appropriately and with understanding.

Think-Aloud Copying Masters included in the Read-Aloud Anthology provide sentence starters to help students "think aloud" about a strategy.

Plays and Choral Readings

Reader's Theater for Building Fluency

You can use the plays and choral readings found at the back of this anthology to perform a Reader's Theater with students. Reading fluency is developed by repeated practice in reading text, especially when the reading is done orally. Reader's Theater can help build students' fluency skills because it engages them in a highly motivating activity that provides an opportunity to read—and reread—text orally. As students practice their assigned sections of the "script," they have multiple opportunities to increase their accuracy in word recognition and their rate of reading. Students are also strongly motivated to practice reading with appropriate phrasing and expression.

Performing Reader's Theater

- Assign speaking roles.

- Do not always assign the speaking role with the most text to the most fluent reader. Readers who need practice reading need ample opportunity to read.

- Have students rehearse by reading and rereading their lines over several days. In these rehearsals, allow time for teacher and peer feedback about pace, phrasing, and expression.

- Students do not memorize their lines, but rather read their lines from the script.

- No sets, costumes, or props are necessary.

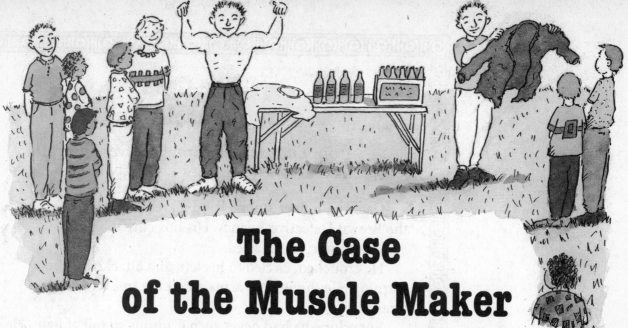

The Case of the Muscle Maker

from *Encyclopedia Brown Solves Them All*

by Donald J. Sobol

Genre: Mystery

Comprehension Strategy: Analyze Story Structure

Think-Aloud Copying Master number 5

Before Reading

Genre: Tell students that you will read aloud a short story that is also a mystery. Explain that a mystery features a problem that needs to be solved or a question that needs to be answered.

Expand Vocabulary: To help students identify the problem and understand the solution in this mystery, introduce the following words:

    bout: a fight

    tussle: to wrestle with something or someone

    tonic: a drink that is intended to improve physical health

    trip-hammer: a power-driven hammer that rises and falls repeatedly

Set a Purpose for Reading: Have students listen carefully and identify the problem and solution.

During Reading

Use the comprehension Think Alouds during the first reading of the story. The note about the genre may be used during subsequent readings.

The Case of the Muscle Maker

from *Encyclopedia Brown Solves Them All*
by Donald J. Sobol

Cadmus Turner stopped and glared at the large tree outside the Brown Detective Agency. His lips curled.

"Arrahhrrr!" he snarled.

He crouched, circled to his left, and attacked without warning. He threw both arms about the tree and began wrestling it.

Encyclopedia had never seen Cadmus so full of fight. He hurried out to the sidewalk for a ringside view.

The bout lasted a minute—till Cadmus's pants fell down. He let go of the tree at once.

"It's a gyp!" he hollered. "I've been robbed."

"It looked like a fair fight till your pants quit," said Encyclopedia. "Next time you tussle the timber, tighten your belt first. You'll win for sure."

"I can't tighten my belt," replied Cadmus. "The ends don't meet any more. I drank four bottles of Hercules's Strength Tonic. I'm ready to bust."

Encyclopedia eyed Cadmus's stomach. It was swollen out like the start of a new continent.

"I should have been able to tear that tree off its roots," said Cadmus.

"Because you drank four bottles of Hercules's Strength Tonic?" asked Encyclopedia.

"Yep," said Cadmus. "Only the stuff doesn't work. I was supposed to feel like Hercules. Instead I feel like a fat slob. And I'm out two dollars!"

"I might get your money back," said Encyclopedia, "if I can prove the tonic is a fake."

"You're hired," said Cadmus. "But I spent all my cash on those four bottles of wish-water. I'll have to pay you later."

Encyclopedia agreed to take the case on faith. Considering the blown-up condition of Cadmus's stomach, it was more an act of mercy than a business deal.[1]

The boys biked to an unused fruit stand on Pine Drive. Cadmus had bought the bottles there earlier that morning.

"Two big kids were setting out boxes of the tonic," said Cadmus. "They told me if I became their first customer, I could have four bottles for the price of two."

"You couldn't say no to a bargain like that," commented Encyclopedia with understanding.

At the fruit stand, a large crowd of children was assembled. Bugs Meany and his Tigers had pushed their way to the front.

The two big boys were about to start the sale. Encyclopedia recognized one of them. He was Wilford Wiggins, a high school dropout. Wilford had more get-rich-quick ideas than tail feathers on a turkey farm.[2] The other boy, a husky youth, was a stranger.

"He's Mike O'Malley," said Cadmus, "from Homestead."

"He looks like he's from Fort Apache," said Encyclopedia. Mike's suit, though it fit perfectly, was wrinkled enough to have gone through an Indian war.

"Gather 'round," shouted Wilford Wiggins. He waved a bottle of Hercules's Strength Tonic. "Gather 'round."

His partner, Mike O'Malley, dropped to the ground and began doing push-ups like a trip-hammer.

"Would you believe Mike weighed only one hundred pounds a year ago?" asked Wilford. "They called him Ribs."

Mike jumped up and removed his suitcoat and shirt. Bare chested, he made muscles in all directions.

"In one short year," bellowed Wilford, "Mike gained a hundred pounds of solid muscle! A miracle, you say? Yes, that's what Hercules's Strength Tonic is—a miracle. The same secret miracle tonic can build a mighty body for each and every boy here today—if," he added hastily, noticing Cadmus and his stomach—"if taken as directed."

Mike was wriggling his huge chest muscles. The battleship tattooed over his heart rolled and pitched.

"See that battleship?" asked Wilford. "Why, a year ago it was nothing but a rowboat! Ahah, hah, hah!"

Bugs Meany held his nose at the joke. "How come you have to sell this wash on the street?" he demanded. "If it's so good, you could sell it in stores."

"A fair question, friend," said Wilford. "I'll give you an honest answer. We need money. We're broke."

Wilford held up Mike's wrinkled suit coat.

"Take a look at this suit coat," Wilford said. "Old and shabby, isn't it? Mike's worn it for two years. Why? Because he didn't

Think Aloud

[2] *I notice that the author introduces Wilford as a character who has many "get-rich-quick ideas." This means Wilford is always thinking of easy ways to make money. If all he wants to do is make money, I wonder if I should believe everything that Wilford says.*

Think Aloud

[3] According to the dialogue, Wilford says you have to drink only a teaspoon of the tonic each day. This seems too good to be true. How can you get muscles from drinking such a small amount?

Genre Study

Short-Story Mystery: The author of this mystery reveals all the clues from the story that should have helped the reader figure out why the tonic was a fake. The reader can reread the story and look for any clues he or she might have missed during the first reading.

think about spending money on himself. He thought only of the powerful body he was going to give every skinny, weak-kneed little shrimp in America!"

Wilford put down the suit coat. He picked up a bottle of Hercules's Strength Tonic again.

"Every cent we had went into developing Mike's wonderful tonic," Wilford continued. "We need money to get the tonic into every store in America! It's a crusade! So I'm cutting the price. You can have four bottles—that's all you need—for half the regular price. Four bottles for a measly two dollars!"

"And I thought he was giving *me* a special price," Cadmus said angrily.

"Forget it," said Encyclopedia. "Look at Bugs."

The Tigers' leader was pop-eyed watching Mike's arm muscles lump, jump, and bump.

"How do you take this tonic?" Bugs asked eagerly.

"One teaspoonful a day," replied Wilford. "Four big bottles like this one will last twelve months. Then you'll have a build like Mike's!"[3]

"I couldn't wait a year," Cadmus muttered. "So I drank the four bottles one after the other. Maybe the stuff works if you follow the directions."

"It doesn't work," said Encyclopedia. "Mike's muscles and Wilford's big sales talk prove it's a fake!"

HOW DID ENCYCLOPEDIA KNOW?

Solution to *The Case of the Muscle Maker*

Wilford Wiggins tried to make the children believe Mike had gained a hundred pounds in one year by drinking Hercules's Strength Tonic.

He also tried to make them believe Mike had been unable to buy a suit because all his money went into developing the tonic.

But the old suit coat still "fit perfectly" on Mike.

If Mike had really gained a hundred pounds in one year, he would have outgrown the suit coat!

When Encyclopedia pointed out this fact to the crowd of children, Wilford had to stop the sale.

And he returned Cadmus's two dollars.

Retell the Story: Have students retell the mystery. Have them add a part to the story where Encyclopedia explains how he knew the tonic was a fake and add Wilford and Mike's reactions to this revelation.

Student Think Aloud

Use Copying Master number 5 to prompt students to share what they observed about the author's placement of clues and the structure of the story.

"I noticed the author used . . ."

Think and Respond

1. What lesson do you think Cadmus learned? *Possible responses: If something seems too good to be true, it probably is; if Cadmus really wants muscles, he needs to work hard and exercise, not just drink a miracle tonic.* **Analytical**

2. What did you learn from reading this story that will help you when you read other mysteries? *Possible responses: I learned to read carefully and look for clues; I will think about what the author says about each character; I will listen to each character's words and decide if he or she is telling the truth.* **Genre**

3. What message do you think the author wants to share with his readers? *Accept reasonable responses. Possible responses: Perhaps he wants us to be more careful and compare what people say to how they act; he wants us to doubt products that seem too good to be true.* **Author's Purpose**

The Fox and the Crane

a fable by Aesop

Genre: Fable

Comprehension Strategy: Analyze Story Structure

Think-Aloud Copying Master number 5

 Before Reading

Genre: Tell students you will read aloud a story based on one of Aesop's fables. Remind students that Aesop was a famous storyteller and that a fable is a story that teaches a lesson. Explain that the main characters in fables are usually animals that talk and act like real people.

Expand Vocabulary: To help students follow the actions of the characters, introduce these words:

> *stalked:* hunted
>
> *shallow:* not very deep
>
> *lap up:* to lick or suck up a liquid, such as water or soup

Set a Purpose for Reading: Have students read to learn about the personalities of the main characters and the moral or lesson of the story.

 **During Reading**

Use the Think Alouds during the first reading of the story. Notes about the genre and cultural perspectives may be used during subsequent readings.

The Fox and the Crane

a fable by Aesop

Once, Fox and Crane were friends.[1] That sounds hard to believe, I know. Remember that they're both hunters, though a fox hunts on land, and a crane in the water. This fox hunted for mice and rabbits in the meadow next to Crane's pond, where she stalked frogs and fish. So they had each noticed the other, and sometimes showed off their catch or just chatted about the weather.

Fox got curious about the food that Crane ate. So he invited her to dinner, hoping that she would invite him to her home in return. He promised to share with her a rabbit he had caught that day. But Fox really wanted to keep the rabbit all for himself, and so he served rabbit soup in very shallow bowls. Fox was able to lap up that soup with his tongue, but Crane could not. She turned her head and twisted her neck, but could only dip the end of her long bill in the bowl. She ate nothing and went home to her pond feeling hungry. As she left, Fox said, "You must not have liked the soup, since you left so much of it. I'm sorry my cooking didn't please you."

"Oh, don't apologize," replied Crane. "Why don't you come for dinner at my place tomorrow?"[2]

Fox caught nothing the next day, so when he arrived at Crane's pond he was hoping for a big meal. Crane welcomed him and quickly served their dinner. It smelled delicious—fish stew, cooked with herbs. But Crane brought the stew to the table in tall jars with long and narrow necks. She could pull out pieces of fish with her long bill, and she ate well. Fox could not get his snout into the neck of his jar. He was so hungry, he forgot his manners and tried pouring the stew out into his mouth. But the pieces of fish blocked the neck. A few drops of broth dribbled out onto his paws, and he licked them up. At the end of the evening, he went home as hungry as Crane had the night before.

"Last night, you apologized, but I'm not apologizing tonight," said Crane. "Let's just say we're even and leave it at that. After all, 'He who plays a trick must be prepared to take a joke.' "

Retell the Story: Have students create a cartoon strip to retell the story. Have them include dialogue for each scene. Invite students to share their cartoon strips with partners.

Student Think Aloud

Use Copying Master number 5 to prompt students to discuss how the author uses things such as character, setting, plot, dialogue, and sequence to tell the story.

"I noticed the author used . . ."

Cultural Perspective

Discuss with students what fables have in common and how the morals, themes, or lessons of these stories apply to people across cultures and times. The stories and characters featured in Aesop's fables can be found in stories from round the world. In the African version of this story, "Anansi and the Turtle," Anansi, the Spider, tricks Turtle out of a dinner and ends up being tricked himself.

Think and Respond

1. What physical differences made it impossible for Fox and Crane to enjoy the meals they served each other? *Possible response: Crane has a long bill or beak, so she could not eat from the bowl. Fox has a wide nose, so he could not eat from the tall jar.* **Analytical**

2. In fables, animals act like people, and in real life we compare people to animals. Sometimes we say someone is "sly as a fox," which means the person is sneaky. How would you describe Crane? *Possible response: Crane is very smart. She played a trick on Fox after she realized that he had played one on her.* **Genre**

3. Explain the moral of the story in your own words. *Possible response: If you trick someone, he or she might also trick you in return.* **Author's Purpose**

Some Rivers

by Frank Asch

Genre: Rhyming Poetry

Poetic Element: Rhythm

Comprehension Strategy: Analyze Text Structure

Think-Aloud Copying Master number 5

Before Reading

Genre: Tell students that you will read a poem about the Florida Everglades. Remind students that not every poem has rhyme, but every poem has rhythm. Rhythm is created by stressed and unstressed syllables.

Expand Vocabulary: Introduce the following words to help students understand the poem:

> *cypress:* a type of tree

> *levee:* a barrier built along a river intended to prevent flooding

Set a Purpose for Reading: For the first reading, have students listen for the sounds of language, rhythm, and rhyme.

During Reading

The sections of the poem that speak about other rivers or express the poet's passionate concern about the Everglades are punctuated by a series of related words. These words, which change the rhythm abruptly, are connected by the word *and*. The vivid action verbs *push*, *tumble*, and *fall* demonstrate the struggle of those other rivers. *Hunters*, *tourists*, and *levee*, all two-syllable nouns accented on the first syllable, are blamed for the damage done to the Everglades, which is described with one-syllable rhyming words: *chain*, *stain*, and *pain*. As you read, pause slightly before each *and* to call attention to these strings of words and accentuate the changes in rhythm.

Some Rivers

by Frank Asch

Some rivers rush to the sea.

They push and tumble and fall.

But the Everglades is a river

with no hurry in her at all.

Soaking the cypress

that grows so tall;

nursing a frog,

so quiet and small;

she flows but a mile

in the course of a day,

with plenty of time

to think on the way.

But how can she cope

with the acres of corn

and sorrowful cities that drain her?[1]

With hunters and tourists and levees

that chain and stain and pain her?

Does the half of her that's left

think only of the past?

Or does she think of her future

and how long it will last?

Some rivers rush to the sea.

They push and tumble and fall.

But the Everglades is a river

with no hurry in her at all.

Set a Purpose for Rereading: Once students have listened for rhyme and rhythm, reread the poem for the purpose of noting alliteration, such as "can," "cope," "acres," and "corn," and exploring imagery and personification.

Student Think Aloud

Use Copying Master number 5 to prompt students to discuss how the structure of the poem affects their understanding of its meaning.

"I noticed the author used . . ."

Cultural Perspective

Native Americans called the Everglades "Grassy Water." Today some people call it "River of Grass."

Think and Respond

1. According to the poem, how is the Everglades different from other rivers? *Possible response: Other rivers move quickly. The Everglades moves slowly.* **Critical**

2. In "Some Rivers" the poet uses rhythm to help suggest the slow progress of the Everglades to the sea. If you were writing a poem about a rainstorm, what kind of rhythm might you want your poem to have? *Possible response: A short staccato rhythm to suggest rain hitting the ground.* **Genre**

3. According to the poet, how are people negatively affecting the Everglades? *Possible responses: Cities are taking water from the river; people are polluting the water.* **Author's Purpose**

PERSISTENCE

by Paul W. Richards

Genre: Autobiography

Comprehension Strategy: Summarize

Think-Aloud Copying Master number 7

Before Reading

Genre: Explain to students that you will be reading aloud an autobiography. Break down the parts of the word *autobiography* as you explain that this text features important events in the author's own life. This means the writer uses words such as *I* and *me*.

Expand Vocabulary: To help students understand the autobiography, introduce the following words:

> *file:* a tool used to carve or cut away
>
> *engineer:* someone who designs or builds things that are useful to people
>
> *persistence:* the act of trying to accomplish a task or reach a goal

Set a Purpose for Reading: Have students listen to find out who Paul W. Richards is and why the title of the selection is "Persistence."

During Reading

Use the Think Alouds during the first reading of the story. Notes about the genre and cultural perspectives may be used during subsequent readings.

PERSISTENCE

by Paul W. Richards

Growing up in Dunmore, Pennsylvania, I was a member of Cub Scout Pack 66. We did many fun projects. One was the Pinewood Derby, a model-car race.

Each Scout made a car from a block of wood. I carved and sanded the wood all by myself. Since my dad did not have many tools, I used a rusty <u>file</u> and some old sandpaper.[1]

My car did not look good. In fact, it was ugly. I tried to cover the scratches and scrapes with paint, but this made it look even worse. I was worried. How would such an ugly car do well?

On race day, many of the other Scouts' cars looked great. I thought I didn't have a chance. To my surprise, my car was the fastest, and I won first place!

The next year, I couldn't wait to race in the Pinewood Derby again. This time, I had help from one of my dad's friends. He used power tools to carve the wood into a smooth curved shape. I decorated it using new paints and stickers. I even used a little toy man as a driver. It really looked like a racecar this time, and I was ready to win first place again.

Unfortunately, I came home disappointed. My car was one of the best-looking cars at the race, but it was also one of the slowest. I lost in the first round.

I never wanted to do another project again. After I had worked so hard to make my car look special, I had still lost.

The next year, my Scout pack had a Space Derby that raced rockets made from blocks of wood. I didn't want to enter, but my mom and dad talked me into it.

I was glad they did. Once I started working on my rocket, I became determined to do my best. This time, I worked as hard sanding and gluing my rocket as I did painting it. I knew now that how it worked was more important than how it looked. Once again, I won first place.

I had learned a valuable lesson, and it had nothing to do with winning. I had learned to be persistent: to keep trying and not to give up. This lesson stayed with me as I grew older.[2]

My childhood dream was to become an astronaut, but people told me it was impossible to achieve that goal. After

Think Aloud

[1] *I can tell that the author is writing about something that happened to him when he was young. He talks about being a Cub Scout and making a racecar out of wood. This is something a child would do.*

Think Aloud

[2] *I think the author summarizes the first part of the text by saying that he learned to be persistent. He will now apply that lesson to the second part of the story. I will read further to find out how the lesson of persistence helped him in the rest of his life.*

Think Aloud

³ *I wonder how he feels now that he is an astronaut. I think he feels proud of himself and his persistence in reaching his goal.*

becoming an engineer, I used persistence to get a job at NASA's Goddard Space Flight Center in Maryland. While I was there, I kept applying to become an astronaut. For eight years, I received rejection letters.

Finally, in 1996, NASA invited me to Houston, Texas. At last, I had been selected to become an astronaut.

On March 8, 2001, I launched aboard the space shuttle Discovery and worked for 12 days in space. This included a trip to the International Space Station and a space walk.

Without *persistence,* my dream would never have come true.³

After Reading

Take Notes: Have students note a key event from the writer's life. Invite students to discuss why the title of the selection is "Persistence."

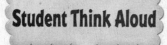

Student Think Aloud

Use Copying Master number 7 to prompt students to share how they would summarize the story and its meaning.

"This was mostly about . . ."

Cultural Perspective

The creation of the International Space Station was truly a global effort. Sixteen nations, including the United States, Russia, Brazil, Japan, Italy, Spain, and Sweden, helped build the station.

Think and Respond

1. The writer says he kept applying to become an astronaut and received rejection letters for eight years. How does this show that he was persistent? *Possible response: Even though he didn't get the job right away, he kept trying and did not give up.* **Analytical**

2. We find out at the end of the selection that the writer grew up to be an astronaut. Why do you think he started his story by describing the racecars and rockets he made as a boy? *Possible response: When he was young, he learned to keep trying. Later in life, this helped him achieve his childhood dream.* **Make Inferences and Analyze**

3. What message do you think Paul W. Richards wants to share with the reader? *Possible responses: He wants people to know that their dreams can come true just like his did; he wants people to see that it is important to work hard and never give up.* **Author's Purpose**

WILD AND SWAMPY

by Jim Arnosky

Genre: Autobiography

Comprehension Strategy: Summarize

Think-Aloud Copying Master number 7

Before Reading

Genre: Tell students that you will read aloud an autobiographical memoir, or a personal narrative. Explain that in this kind of writing, the writer describes experiences that actually happened to him. The writer also reflects, or looks back on, the topic and shares his thoughts and feelings.

Expand Vocabulary: Introduce these words to students before reading:

> *leaching:* removing material by soaking in water
>
> *planks:* wooden boards
>
> *canal:* a narrow waterway
>
> *scurried:* ran in quick little steps

Set a Purpose for Reading: Ask students to listen for words the writer uses to describe the swamp and to reveal how he feels about it.

During Reading

Use the Think Alouds during the first reading of the text. Notes about the genre may be used during subsequent readings.

Wild and Swampy

by Jim Arnosky

Sheltered from the wind by tree trunks, branches, and leaves, the water in a swamp can be as still as glass. Stained from black rotting vegetation and by the reddish-brown tannic acid leaching out of tree bark, swamp water is dark and highly reflective. Every swamp scene is really two scenes—one upright, one upside-down.[1]

The stillness in a swamp can actually help you locate wildlife. Any disturbance in the water is most likely being made by an animal.

I always feel a mixture of excitement and caution when I'm in a swamp—especially a southern swamp. The animals that are abundantly found in the warm South are those I see least often in my cool northern hills. I'm talking about snakes—nonvenomous and venomous, small and large. One southern brown water snake was five feet long and as thick as my upper arm. That's a great big water snake![2]

The nonvenomous brown water snake is the snake most often mistaken for a venomous cottonmouth moccasin. It's easy to see why. The two snakes are found in the same places. They have similar markings, and both have triangular heads.

In the cypress swamp Deanna and I followed a narrow boardwalk that led us deeper and deeper into the silence. The only sounds we heard were our own footsteps on the wooden planks. Then, somewhere in the distance, a barred owl called, "Who-hoo-hoo-hoooooo." All around us we saw only trees and water until another barred owl, perched right above us in a tupelo-gum tree, hooted back, "Who-hoo-hoo-hoooooo."

Barred owls are found in many swamps. Their call, which sounds like someone asking, "Who cooks for you?" is a familiar swamp sound.[3] This owl called again, then spread its wings and flew noiselessly to another perch. When most owls are sleeping, these swamp-dwelling owls are wide-awake, hunting all day long. When do they sleep?

Where I live, raccoons are night creatures. But in the southern swamplands, raccoons hunt during the day, when they are less likely to bump into a hungry alligator. Alligators normally feed after dark.

Genre Study

Memoir/Personal Narrative: In a memoir, the writer often looks back at an earlier time with mixed emotions. In this selection, the writer feels happiness because he is spending time in a place he enjoys, but he also expresses sadness because he knows that eventually he has to leave and go back home.

One day in Georgia, in Okefenokee Swamp, I saw a raccoon wading in a canal. At one point the raccoon waded right by a large alligator half-hidden on the grassy bank. The alligator immediately began crawling toward the raccoon. Unaware that it was being stalked, the raccoon stopped to fish in the water with its front paws. The alligator froze in its muddy tracks. The raccoon began to wade again. The alligator followed, inching closer and closer. When it was within striking distance of the raccoon, the alligator sank itself deeper into the greenery, getting ready to rush forward. Some dry grass rustled. The raccoon heard and scurried away.

Raccoons, opossums, otters, bobcats, black bear, and deer all thrive in swampland. But seeing these mammals in a swamp is much more difficult than seeing the reptiles and birds. Mammals do not sun themselves in the open the way reptiles do. Nor do they draw attention to themselves by sudden movements or loud sounds the way birds do. Every mammal sighting in a swamp is a surprise.

To keep their fur from becoming waterlogged, swamp-dwelling mammals must make use of every little bit of higher ground. Even a clump of matted grass can be a dry island for a wet and weary swamp mammal.

Sometimes I simply cannot leave a place. In the mangrove swamp I always stay until the last light and wish the day was longer. There is so much more I want to see—more swamps and covered miles of watery ground.

After Reading

Take Notes: Have students list three interesting details they learned about southern swamps and the animals that live in them. Help students by reading aloud passages again, as necessary.

Student Think Aloud

Use Copying Master number 7 to prompt students to share how they would summarize the information presented in this article.

"This was mostly about . . ."

Think and Respond

1. How do you think the author learned so much about swamps? *Possible responses: He has visited many swamps; he may have read articles about swamp animals.* **Inferential**

2. A memoir includes the author's personal feelings about a topic. List one example from the text that shows how Jim Arnosky feels about wild and swampy places. *Possible responses: I always feel a mixture of excitement and caution when I'm in a swamp; Sometimes I simply cannot leave a place; I always stay until the last light.* **Genre**

3. Why do you think Jim Arnosky chose to write about visiting a swamp? *Accept reasonable responses. Possible responses: It might be one of his favorite places and he wants to share his excitement with others. He may want people to appreciate swamps as places teeming with wildlife.* **Author's Purpose**

Take Me Out to the Ball Game!

lyrics by Jack Norworth *(1927 version)*

Genre: Poetry/Song

Comprehension Strategy: Monitor Comprehension

Think-Aloud Copying Master number 8

Before Reading

Genre: Explain to students that you will be reading aloud the lyrics, or words, to a song that is popular at baseball games. Remind students that song lyrics can change slightly over time and point out that this version is from 1927. Even though students will probably recognize the familiar refrain, or repeating stanza, they may be surprised to learn about the larger context or story that is told in the rest of the song.

Expand Vocabulary: Introduce the following words before reading:

> *Coney Isle:* a popular amusement park in Coney Island, New York City.
>
> *fret:* to worry
>
> *root:* to cheer for a team

Set a Purpose for Reading: Have students listen to find out who Nelly Kelly is and how she is connected to a popular song sung at baseball games throughout the United States.

During Reading

Use the comprehension Think Alouds during the first reading of the story. Notes about the genre and cultural perspective may be used during subsequent readings.

Take Me Out to the Ball Game!

lyrics by Jack Norworth (*1927 version*)

Nelly Kelly loved baseball games,
Knew the players, knew all their names,
You could see her there ev'ry day,
Shout "Hurray" when they'd play.
Her boyfriend by the name of Joe
Said, "To Coney Isle, dear, let's go,"
Then Nelly started to fret and pout,
And to him I heard her shout.[1]

"Take me out to the ball game,
Take me out with the crowd.
Buy me some peanuts and Cracker Jack,
I don't care if I never get back,
Let me root, root, root for the home team,
If they don't win it's a shame.
For it's one, two, three strikes, you're out,
At the old ball game."

Nelly Kelly was sure some fan,
She would root just like any man,
Told the umpire he was wrong,
All along, good and strong.
When the score was just two to two,
Nelly Kelly knew what to do,
Just to cheer up the boys she knew,
She made the game sing this song.[2]

"Take me out to the ball game,
Take me out with the crowd.
Buy me some peanuts and Cracker Jack,
I don't care if I never get back,
Let me root, root, root for the home team,
If they don't win it's a shame.
For it's one, two, three strikes, you're out,
At the old ball game."

Think Aloud

[1] *I did not know the context of this popular song, so before I read the familiar refrain, I will re-read the first part of the song to be sure I know who is shouting and why. I learn that Nelly would rather go to the game than Coney Isle.*

Think Aloud

[2] *I notice that when the score of the game is tied, Nelly starts singing. I think she does this to encourage the players and show her support.*

Reread or Sing the Song: After you reread (or sing) the song, discuss the sounds of the language in the text. Discuss with students how the rhythm and beat in lines such as *Let me root, root, root for the home team* emphasize the meaning and the emotion. Then ask students to clap the stacatto beats (root, root, root) and spread their arms for the held words (home, team) as you reread the refrain.

Student Think Aloud

Use Copying Master 8 to prompt students to share the strategies they used to monitor their comprehension throughout the song.

> "When I read _____, I had to reread, read back, read on . . ."

Cultural Perspective

Although many people think of baseball as a uniquely American game, it is really a modern version of stick-and-ball games that people have been playing for centuries. People from the ancient cultures of Persia, Egypt, and Greece used a stick and a ball to play games for fun and as part of some ceremonies.

Think and Respond

1. How can you tell Nelly is a true baseball fan? *Possible responses: Nelly would rather go to a baseball game than an amusement park; Nelly yells at the umpire when he makes a bad call against her team; she sings to cheer up her team.* **Inferential**

2. What details in the refrain would appeal to baseball fans and make them want to sing the song? *Possible response: The lyrics talk about things people enjoy doing at baseball games, like eating snacks and cheering for your team.* **Genre**

3. Why do you think Jack Norworth wrote this song? *Accept reasonable responses. Possible response: Perhaps he wanted to show that baseball is all-American and appeals to everyone.* **Author's Purpose**

The Present from France

by Carla Stevens

Genre: Historical Fiction

Comprehension Strategy: Monitor Comprehension

Think-Aloud Copying Master number 8

Before Reading

Genre: Tell students that you will read aloud an excerpt from a historical novel. Explain that historical fiction combines a real event—in this case, the creation of the Statue of Liberty—with imaginary characters.

Expand Vocabulary: Introduce the following words before reading to help students better understand the historical context of the selection:

> *parlor:* a living room
>
> *peered:* looked intently
>
> *pedestal:* the base of a statue
>
> *super:* a caretaker of an apartment building (short for superintendent)

Set a Purpose for Reading: Have students listen to find out what Lily's problem is and how her family tries to help her solve it.

During Reading

Use the comprehension Think Alouds during the first reading of the story. Notes about the genre and cultural perspective may be used during subsequent readings.

Think Aloud

[1] *When I think of the Statue of Liberty, I think of a finished monument. As I reread and read ahead, I learn that the statue actually consists of hundreds of pieces that were made in France, traveled across the ocean on a ship, and were then put together here in the United States.*

The Present from France

by Carla Stevens

It was almost time for supper. Grandma was feeding baby Charlie, and Mama was cooking cabbage on the big coal-burning stove. After Lily set the table, she went into the parlor to read the book she had brought from school.

Papa was sitting in his favorite armchair, reading a magazine.

"Look, Lily," he said. "Look at the picture of the French ship that is bringing the Statue of Liberty to New York. It is due here in just a few more days."

Lily sat on the arm of Papa's chair and peered at the picture in the magazine. "But where is Miss Liberty?" she asked. "I don't see her."

"Below deck, packed in hundreds of boxes," Papa replied. "It will be some time before we can see her. First we have to build the pedestal for her to stand on."[1]

"Mama doesn't like Miss Liberty," Lily said.

Mr. Lafferty put down his magazine. "Oh, I'm sure she does."

"No, she doesn't," Lily insisted. "She says we shouldn't have to pay for it."

"We don't have to pay for the statue, Lily. The statue is a gift from France," Papa said. "We only have to raise enough money to pay for the pedestal."

"But she says the pedestal will cost a lot of money. She thinks we should use our money to help feed poor people instead."

Mr. Lafferty picked up his magazine again. "Goodness, Lily, why bother your head about all this?"

"Our class is raising money for the pedestal and I didn't put in anything again today," Lily said. "I was almost the only one."

"Well, well, Lily, that's a problem, isn't it."

"Supper is ready!" called Mrs. Lafferty.

Lily and Papa went into the kitchen. Lily sat down at the big round table next to Grandma. Mama began dishing out the corned beef and cabbage.

Papa took a bite of cabbage. "Mmm. What a good cook you are, Mama!"

Mrs. Lafferty smiled at her husband.

"Lily tells me that her class is raising money for Miss Liberty's pedestal," he said. "Can't we think of some way for Lily to earn a little money, too?"

Mama set her mouth in a straight line. "All the poor people living in this city! No one thinks of raising money to help them!"[2]

"I know, I know," Papa said. "But what a wonderful statue Miss Liberty is! And someday soon she will stand in our harbor to welcome all the immigrants like ourselves who have come to America seeking a better life and the freedom to enjoy it."

"Humpf," Mama said. "You talk about freedom. But freedom won't fill an empty stomach."[3]

"Sometimes freedom is more important than an empty stomach, Mama."

"You don't remember what it feels like to be hungry, Papa. I remember."

Grandma glanced at Lily. "All this talk isn't helping Lily," she said. "How is she going to earn money for Miss Liberty's pedestal?"

"Maybe you can help Mrs. Casella in her grocery store," Papa suggested.

"Or maybe you could help Otto, the super, sweep the front steps of our apartment building," Grandma said.

Papa pushed back his chair and stood up. "That was a good dinner, Mama." He turned to Lily. "Tomorrow is Saturday. I'm sure you will find something to do for Miss Liberty, Lily."

Think Aloud

[2]*I figured out that Lily's problem is that her class is raising money to pay for the pedestal, but she has not been a part of it. She has not given any money because her mother does not think it's for a worthy cause.*

Think Aloud

[3]*I think Lily's mother is a practical woman. She thinks raising money to feed poor people is more important than paying for a statue that she feels won't help anyone. I can understand the way she feels.*

Retell the Story: Invite students to retell the events of the story. Use the opportunity to discuss the problem and solution in the story. Ask students how they would solve Lilly's problem and explain what they think of the points that Mama and Papa make.

Student Think Aloud

Use Copying Master number 8 to prompt students to share strategies for monitoring comprehension, especially in sections with large amounts of dialogue.

"When I read _____, I had to reread, read back, read on . . ."

Cultural Perspective

In America, one of the major supporters of the fundraising effort for the pedestal was businessman and publisher Joseph Pulitzer. As an immigrant from Hungary himself, he understood the importance of creating a symbol to recognize a country where people from all cultures are free to follow their dreams.

Think and Respond

1. Why does Papa think raising money for the pedestal is a good idea? *Possible response: Papa says the Statue of Liberty will be an important symbol of freedom.* **Inferential**

2. How might this story change if it were set in the present? *Possible responses: The story would feature a different monument; the parts of the monument might not come on a boat but on a plane.* **Genre**

3. It is clear that Mama and Papa don't agree on the importance of raising money for the pedestal. How does the author let you know that Papa is trying to "keep the peace" with Mama? *Possible responses: He keeps complimenting Mama on the dinner she cooked; he tries to help Lily find ways to earn the money on her own rather than argue with Mama about it.* **Author's Purpose**

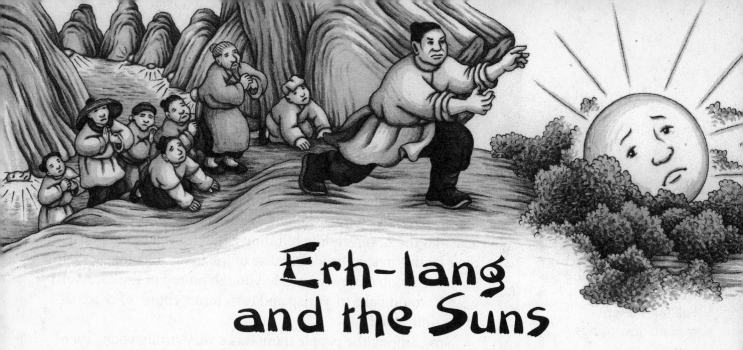

Erh-lang and the Suns

by M. A. Jagendorf and Virginia Weng

Genre: Folktale

Comprehension Strategy: Monitor Comprehension

Think-Aloud Copying Master number 8

Before Reading

Genre: Remind students that a folktale is a story that has been told and retold for many, many years. This particular retelling is from China. Like other folktales, there are other versions of the story from different countries and different cultures.

Expand Vocabulary: Introduce the following words to help students follow the action and characters in this folktale:

> *glare:* blinding light
>
> *fling:* to throw with force
>
> *plague:* something that causes great harm or disease
>
> *cautiously:* carefully

Set a Purpose for Reading: Invite students to listen to find out who Erh-lang was and how he helped his people.

During Reading

Use the comprehension Think Alouds during the first reading of the story. Notes about the genre and cultural perspective may be used during subsequent readings.

Erh-lang and the Suns

by M. A. Jagendorf and Virginia Weng

In the time before anything and everything, there were Seven Suns in the land of China. They shone without end and there was neither day nor night. People suffered cruelly from the heat and the never-ending blinding light. They could not farm their land or rest in peace because of the fierce burning glare. If they put a blob of newly kneaded dough on top of the courtyard wall, it would bake to a crisp and turn into a chunk of charcoal in no time at all!

Now, among the people there was a very strong young man named Erh-lang. Erh-lang was stronger than fifty men. He could lift mountains with his hands and would fling great rock boulders to the sky just to show how strong he was. Everyone admired him.[1]

One day the wise men came together to speak of the terror of the Seven Suns. Said one of the wise men: "Let us ask Erh-lang to help us in our sad trouble. He is the only one who can conquer these blinding, blistering Suns."

Everyone thought this a good idea, and seven of the oldest men were sent to ask Erh-lang for help.

When they came to him, he was rolling giant gray boulders along the dry land.

"We have come to you, Erh-lang," the oldest said, "to beg you to rid us of the terrible plague in our land. I speak of the Seven Suns that blind us with their light and burn us with their heat."[2]

"I know how you suffer," said Erh-lang, "for I, too, am troubled by their never-ending burning and never-ending light. I will gladly help you, and I will start at once."

The old men thanked him and wished him luck.

Erh-lang kept his word. He began by watching the Seven Suns carefully. Soon he noticed that they did not come up together, but that they followed one upon the other.

"That is fine," he thought. "Getting one at a time will be much easier."

He walked up to a rocky mountain nearby and slowly tilted it to one side, leaving a deep hole in the earth. Then he waited for a Sun to rise. Soon it came out of the east, filling the sky and land with glaring light. Erh-lang dashed up, spread his huge arms wide, took hold of the giant hot Sun, and, rushing to the mountain he had tilted sideways, threw the Sun into the hole underneath. Holding down the Sun with his giant boot, he pushed the mountain on top of it.

"Now there is one less burning glare. That was easy. I'll get ready for the next Sun."

He looked around and saw another big, rocky mountain, rolled it aside, leaning it carefully on its own weight, again making a deep hole in the earth.

He rested and waited. After a time, the heat and light told of the coming of the next Sun. No sooner was it out from the east than Erh-lang leaped at it, got hold of it with his gigantic arms, and flung it into the hole under the mountain. Holding down this Sun, too, with his giant boot, he dragged the mountain over it and covered it.

"Now two of these misery-makers are gone," he said, waving his arms in the air. He rested for a time and then he raised another mountain, caught another Sun, and buried it. He did this to three other Suns until there was just one left.

Now, Seventh Sun had seen what had happened to his six brothers. He had seen one after another disappear and he was greatly worried. He was almost afraid to climb out of the east.

In the end he did. Cautiously and slowly, he crept up . . . and, seeing a plant nearby, hid under it, hoping Erh-lang would not see him. But Erh-lang did see him, for the Seventh Sun could not hide his light or his heat.[3]

Erh-lang had pushed aside a mountain to bury Seventh Sun. Now he rushed up, ready for his task. But Seventh Sun began to weep and begged, "Please don't bury me under the mountain, powerful Erh-lang, as you have my brothers. I will stop giving terrible heat and blinding light. Only don't bury me under the mountain."

People had gathered around Erh-lang. They felt sorry for Seventh Sun and joined in the begging.

"Be kind, Erh-lang," pleaded Seventh Sun.

"I will not bury you, Seventh Sun, if you promise to shine for only a part of the day so that the people can rest without your heat and your awful glare the rest of the time."

"I promise, I swear," cried Seventh Sun, "I swear, only don't bury me under the mountain."

Erh-lang's heart had softened, as had the hearts of the people.

Think Aloud

[3] I didn't expect Seventh Sun to seem human and be able to think. He must try to escape Erh-lang since he knows what happened to his brothers.

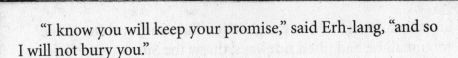

"I know you will keep your promise," said Erh-lang, "and so I will not bury you."

Erh-lang let Seventh Sun come up from under the plant to give light and warmth to the people during the day.

And since the light and heat were not there all the time, for the Sun would set by nightfall, it was a benefit to all—both to the earth and to man.

Ever since then, Seventh Sun would not harm the plant that had given him shelter. No matter how long that plant is in the sunshine, it does not dry up. Folks call it "Water-Leaf Plant" (*shui-yeh-ts'ai*), for it is always lush, green, and soft. And to this day it is still the people's favorite wild-growing vegetable.

After Reading

Retell the Story: Have students create a cartoon strip to illustrate the story. Have them include dialogue for each scene. Invite students to share their cartoon strips with partners.

Student Think Aloud

Use Copying Master number 8 to prompt students to share how they monitored their comprehension while reading the folktale.

"When I read _____, I had to reread, read back, read on . . ."

Cultural Perspective

Pourquoi tales that explain day and night are common among the cultures of the world, but in some versions the world begins only with night and no day. Have students compare the theme of other day/night stories they know. Ask them to explain why such stories are universal to most cultures. A story from the Kamayura of Brazil tells of people starving because it is too dark to hunt, fish, or plant crops. The people finally discover that birds possess the day, and light comes to them in the form of the brightly colored feathers of the red macaw.

Think and Respond

1. How does Erh-lang show intelligence when he takes on the task of getting rid of the Seven Suns? *Possible responses: He watches the Seven Suns and studies what they do so he can form a plan of attack. He deals with each sun, one at a time, so it is easier to conquer all the suns.* **Analytical**

2. Why is it necessary that Erh-lang take pity on Seventh Sun for this folktale to explain night and day? *Possible response: If Erh-lang had buried Seventh Sun, the folktale would no longer have explained how day and night were created.* **Genre**

3. How do the authors show that Erh-lang is a hero or a character who displays positive traits? *Possible responses: Erh-lang agrees to use his strength to help his people and end their suffering; Erh-lang is kind to Seventh Sun and agrees to let him shine for part of the day.* **Author's Purpose**

What REA Service Means to Our Farm Home

by Rose Dudley Scearce
Member, *Shelby (Kentucky) Rural Electric Cooperative*

Genre: Nonfiction/Persuasive

Comprehension Strategy: Analyze Text Structure

Think-Aloud Copying Master number 5

Before Reading

Genre: Help students better understand this selection by providing some historical background information. Explain that during the Great Depression of the 1920s and 1930s, only about ten percent of Americans living in rural areas had electricity. President Franklin D. Roosevelt created the Rural Electrification Administration (REA), which offered loans to build power plants and extend power lines. Farmers could also receive money to help them put electricity in their homes and barns. Explain that this article was written by a Kentucky woman at that time.

Expand Vocabulary: Explain the following words before reading to help students better understand the selection:

> *cooperative:* a group of farmers who work together by sharing supplies
>
> *sentiments:* feelings or opinions
>
> *overshoes:* boots worn over regular shoes
>
> *pike:* a road (short for "turnpike")

Set a Purpose for Reading: Have students listen to learn about this time in history and how electricity changed the writer's life.

During Reading

Use the comprehension Think Alouds during the first reading of the story. Notes about the genre may be used during subsequent readings.

What REA Service Means to Our Farm Home

by Rose Dudley Scearce
Member, Shelby (Kentucky) Rural Electric Cooperative

The first benefit we received from the REA service was lights, and aren't lights grand? My little boy expressed my sentiments when he said, "Mother, I didn't realize how dark our house was until we got electric lights." We had been reading by an Aladdin lamp and thought it was good, but it didn't compare with our I. E. S. reading lamp. Are all of you reading by an I. E. S. lamp? If you are not, get one tomorrow. When you compare how much easier on your eyes an I. E. S. lamp is than an ordinary electric lamp, you will not hesitate, especially when you find they do not cost any more than an ordinary lamp. The I. E. S. lamps are not made by just one company but are lamps approved by the Illuminating Engineering Society.

Recently I read in the Rural Electrification NEWS that the radio was the most popular appliance that had been bought. So, like the rest of the people, we changed our storage-battery radio into an electric radio. This was our next benefit.[1]

Next we bought an electric refrigerator. Of course, next after a refrigerator comes making ice cream in the trays. We changed our washing machine from a machine driven by gasoline to one driven by the electric current as our next improvement. The machine was all right with gasoline, but, my, the noise it made! It is such a blessed relief to do the laundry in peace and quiet. We changed our pump for the pressure tank in our bathroom and water system from a hand pump to an electric pump. I did not buy an electric iron at first, as I do not do my own ironing. I was impressed, when I did, at how much improved irons were since I moved to the country. I can turn my dial on the iron to any fabric I may be ironing and the iron will stay the temperature needed for the fabric until I move the dial. The next benefit we received from the current was our electric stove. We were so anxious for the current that we wired our house many months before the current was turned on, and we wired our kitchen for an electric range.[2]

Think Aloud

[1] *When I read the words "first" and "next," I understand that the author is using sequence words to structure the article. This helps me to keep track of the points she makes.*

Think Aloud

[2] *I wonder how irons and stoves worked before electricity. They probably didn't stay hot for long.*

If you follow the directions in the cook book given you with your range, that is, use very little water in cooking, use a covered pan as big as your heating unit, and use your "free heat," you will be surprised at how little electricity you will burn.

Before the current was turned on, when anyone asked me what appliance I wanted most I always said that I wanted a vacuum cleaner. I do not know what kind of a person you are, but I expect that you are a nice, neat person and that when it rains you put on your <u>overshoes</u> on the porch before you go out and take the muddy overshoes off on the porch before you come into the house.[3] We don't do that way at our house. We rush out when it rains without overshoes, and when we come in we wipe half the mud on the mat at the door and the other half we wipe on my living-room carpet. I have an old-fashioned body Brussells carpet on my living-room floor, and when I swept it I raised as much dust as if I had been sweeping the dusty <u>pike</u>. When I finished I was choking with the dust, the carpet was not clean, and I was in a bad humor. Now with the vacuum cleaner, I can even dust the furniture before I clean the carpet, the carpet gets clean, and I stay in a good humor.

So you see I am thoroughly enjoying the many things that electricity had made possible, and I am enjoying life more because I have more time to spend visiting my friends, studying and reading, and doing the things that make life richer and fuller.

Think Aloud

[3] *I wonder why the author writes as if she is talking to one person. It sounds like she is having a conversation with someone. Maybe she does this to sound friendly.*

After Reading

Take Notes: Have students make a list of all the new appliances the author purchased once she had electricity in her home. Help students by reading aloud the relevant passages.

Student Think Aloud

Use Copying Master number 5 to prompt students to share their thoughts on how and why the author structures her article the way she does.

"I noticed the author used..."

Cultural Perspective

As you discuss the historical aspects of the article, draw students' attention to some of the descriptive passages (changing from a gas-powered washing machine to an electric one). Ask students to think about such dramatic changes in their lifetime.

Think and Respond

1. Why do you think the writer buys so many appliances? *Possible responses: Everything is new to her, so she is excited to try out all the appliances; the new appliances make her work easier.* **Inferential**

2. How can you tell that this article is not meant only to inform readers? *Possible responses: The writer describes the benefits that she received from having electricity for the first time; the writer is sharing her personal experiences, not trying to give facts or explain something.* **Genre**

3. Why do you think the author wrote this article? *Possible response: She wrote this to describe how much better her life is now that she has electricity.* **Author's Purpose**

A Word to the Wise

by Mari Paz Pradillo

Genre: Rhyming Poetry

Poetic Element: Imagery

Comprehension Strategy: Analyze Text Structure

Think-Aloud Copying Master number 5

Before Reading

Genre: Tell students that you will read aloud a poem that is really one long riddle. Explain that the poet uses imagery to provide clues to help readers solve the riddle. Imagery describes how the author uses words to create a picture in the reader's mind.

Expand Vocabulary: Introduce the following words before reading to help students comprehend the imagery:

> *den:* a place where an animal sleeps or rests
>
> *agile:* able to move quickly and easily
>
> *coil:* a spiral or loop

Set a Purpose for Reading: Have students listen carefully to form a picture in their minds of who or what the speaker in the poem is. Point out that they may have to adjust their mental image each time a new clue is given.

During Reading

Read slowly and pause after each stanza to help students think about the new information or clues. Then reread, pausing to draw students' attention to the comprehension Think Aloud and the genre note.

A Word to the Wise

by Mari Paz Pradillo

I don't have to study.
I don't go to school.
I know what I know,
And I'm nobody's fool.

I hatched from an egg
And I live in a <u>den</u>,
But I'm hardly a lion,
A fox, or a hen.[1]

I don't have a nose,
So I smell with my tongue.
I'm <u>agile</u> and mobile,
Though I can't fly or run.

I have no paws
To leave tracks or trails.
I'm not a fish, though
I'm covered with scales.

My cheeks help me locate
A meal I can't see,
But it feels like a meal.
It's much warmer than me.

I roll up in a <u>coil</u>.
It comes close. I am still.
I will swallow it whole.
I will bite. I will kill.

Some think me cruel.
I have style. I have skill.
I'm the colors of jewels
And survive, that I will.

So leave me alone
And this tale you will tell:
Snake rules at ground level.
Watch your heels and farewell.

Think Aloud

[1] *I like the way each stanza provides some clues. I want to try to solve the riddle after each one. Then I read on to get the next clues. This structure makes the poem more interesting and entertaining.*

Genre Study

Poetry: This poem uses an ABCB rhyming pattern. Only the second and fourth lines of each stanza rhyme.

After Reading

Set a Purpose for Rereading: Have students make a list of the clues that helped them solve the riddle and identify the animal. They can make two columns—one for clues that tell what the animal is, and one for clues that tell what it is *not*—to show how the poet uses both kinds of sentences.

Student Think Aloud

Use Copying Master number 5 to prompt students to share how the author used the elements of poetry to tell this riddle.

> "I noticed the author used . . ."

Cultural Perspective

Despite their bad reputations, snakes have held positions of honor in many cultures throughout the world. Cobras were worshipped in ancient times as the form of Wadjit, cobra goddess of Lower Egypt. In India, cobras are still considered a sacred animal and are honored at an annual festival.

Think and Respond

1. Why do you think the poem is titled "A Word to the Wise"? *Possible response: The speaker of the poem is a snake and it is warning people to be careful of its presence. It might also refer to the fact that wise people who think about the words will be able to figure out the riddle.* **Analytical**

2. How does the poet create a riddle out of a poem? *Possible responses: She gives you information about the snake in bits and pieces of imagery throughout the poem; some of the clues can refer to more than one thing or animal; you have to put the clues together to solve the riddle.* **Genre**

3. Why do you think the poet wrote this poem? *Possible responses: I think she wrote it just for fun; I think she wanted to challenge people to read the poem and solve the riddle.* **Author's Purpose**

Amazing Animals

by Maryalice Yakutchik and Adrienne Mason

Genre: Nonfiction/Expository

Comprehension Strategy: Generate Questions

Think-Aloud Copying Master number 1

Before Reading

Genre: Tell students that you will read aloud several short nonfiction news stories that all focus on animals. Remind students that the subjects of nonfiction/expository pieces are real people, things, or events.

Expand Vocabulary: To help students follow the expository text, introduce these words before reading:

> *fawning:* giving great amounts of attention to
>
> *predator:* an animal that hunts other animals for food
>
> *enclosure:* an area surrounded by walls or fences, commonly found in a zoo
>
> *stray:* a lost or homeless animal

Set a Purpose for Reading: Have students listen to the three short selections and think about how they are similar.

During Reading

Use the comprehension Think Alouds during the first reading of the story. Notes about the genre and cultural perspective may be used during subsequent readings.

Amazing Animals

Yes, Deer

by Maryalice Yakutchik

DATELINE: Wiesbaden, Germany

Mädchen, the German shepherd mix, sure didn't mind <u>fawning</u> all over her new friend. Maybe it was because her new friend was a baby deer! Animal control officers brought the orphaned fawn to Lydia Weber, who was known for adopting animals. But it was her dog who really took over the mothering. Mädchen started by licking the deer—now called Mausi—from head to toe. And when Mausi wouldn't drink milk from a bottle, Weber held the bottle under Mädchen so that the fawn would feel like it was nursing from its mother. No matter what, Mausi's bond to her doggie mom will always be "en-deer-ing"![1]

Spotty Friendship

by Adrienne Mason

DATELINE: Antoli, Gujarat, India[2]

A leopard seems to think it's supposed to be friends with cows—not eat them. Villagers spotted the <u>predator</u> making regular nighttime visits to a local cow living in a sugarcane field. The two snuggle together, and the cow licks the leopard's head and neck. Although dogs bark nonstop when the leopard shows up, villagers welcome the big cat. Since the visits started, other animals that might damage crops have stayed away, fearing the leopard. For now, wildlife officials are leaving the cat alone. Looks like a leopard sometimes *can* change its spots.

The Odd Couple

by Maryalice Yakutchik

DATELINE:

Berlin, Germany

Muschi the cat may have lost one of her nine lives after she fell into a bear <u>enclosure</u> at a zoo several years ago. But her new friend Mäusschen the bear let her keep the rest of them! Becoming best buds, the 100-pound Asiatic black bear and the 10-pound cat cuddle together in the sun, curl up for catnaps, and even share food such as fish, chicken, and fruit.[3] "But sometimes Muschi steals the chicken," says Heiner Klös, deputy director at the Berlin Zoological Gardens.

No one knows why the bear and cat became friends. One reason may be that 34-year-old Mäusschen is just too old to chase away the <u>stray</u>. Or maybe she wants a friend—one that purrs instead of growls!

Genre Study

Nonfiction/ Expository: The article includes a quotation from a real person, the deputy director of the zoo. This expert adds credibility and interest to the story.

Think Aloud

[3] *I think this is an unusual story about two animals that would not normally be friends. The author gives several examples that describe how they act toward each other.*

After Reading

Summarize: Reread the three articles. Have students summarize the key information in each article.

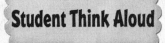

Use Copying Master number 1 to prompt students to share a question they have about the unusual animal relationships described in these selections.

"I wonder . . ."

Cultural Perspective

The Berlin Zoological Gardens opened in 1844 and has grown to become the world's largest zoo. It is the oldest zoo in Germany and is home to more than 14,000 animals and over 1,700 species.

Think and Respond

1. What do all three articles have in common? *Possible response: They all describe friendships between two animals that are typically enemies.* **Analytical**

2. What details do the writers include to add interest to their articles? *Possible response: The first writer describes how the dog cleans the deer by licking it. In the third article, the writer describes things the cat and bear do together, like take naps and share food.* **Genre**

3. Why do you think these three articles were written? Do you think the authors wanted to inform, entertain or persuade? Remember that authors often have more than one purpose. *Possible response: The writers wanted to inform, but they also wanted to entertain because they include some funny details.* **Author's Purpose**

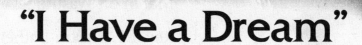

"I Have a Dream"

excerpt from a speech given at the
March on Washington, 1963

by Rev. Dr. Martin Luther King, Jr.

Genre: Persuasive Speech

Comprehension Strategy: Generate Questions

Think-Aloud Copying Master number 1

Before Reading

Genre: Explain that in a persuasive speech, the writer's goal is to convince the audience to accept his or her opinion about a topic. This selection is from the speech delivered by Rev. Dr. Martin Luther King, Jr. to an audience of 200,000 people at the Lincoln Memorial as part of the March on Washington for Jobs and Freedom. Remind students that they will be listening to an excerpt from the entire speech.

Expand Vocabulary: To help students appreciate the prose, take time to introduce and explain these challenging words before reading the selection:

> *momentous:* of great importance
>
> *manacles:* handcuffs
>
> *languished:* lived under conditions that caused a loss of health or vitality
>
> *prodigious:* extraordinarily large, magnificent

Set a Purpose for Reading: Invite students to think about the speaker's purpose as they listen to the language and word choice.

During Reading

Use the comprehension Think Alouds during the first reading of the speech. Notes about the genre and cultural perspective may be used during subsequent readings.

"I Have a Dream"

excerpt from a speech given at the
March on Washington, 1963

by Rev. Dr. Martin Luther King, Jr.

I am happy to join with you today in what will go down in history as the greatest demonstration for freedom in the history of our nation.

Five score years ago, a great American, in whose symbolic shadow we stand today, signed the Emancipation Proclamation. This <u>momentous</u> decree came as a great beacon light of hope to millions of Negro slaves who had been seared in the flames of withering injustice. It came as a joyous daybreak to end the long night of their captivity.

But one hundred years later, the Negro still is not free. One hundred years later, the life of the Negro is still sadly crippled by the <u>manacles</u> of segregation and the chains of discrimination. One hundred years later, the Negro lives on a lonely island of poverty in the midst of a vast ocean of material prosperity. One hundred years later, the Negro is still <u>languished</u> in the corners of American society and finds himself an exile in his own land. And so we've come here today to dramatize a shameful condition. . . .

And as we walk, we must make the pledge that we shall always march ahead. We cannot turn back. There are those who are asking the devotees of civil rights, "When will you be satisfied?"

. . . We can never be satisfied as long as our bodies, heavy with the fatigue of travel, cannot gain lodging in the motels of the highways and the hotels of the cities.[1] We cannot be satisfied as long as the Negro's basic mobility is from a smaller ghetto to a larger one. We can never be satisfied as long as our children are stripped of their selfhood and robbed of their dignity by signs stating "for whites only." We cannot be satisfied as long as a Negro in Mississippi cannot vote and a Negro in New York believes he has nothing for which to vote. No, no, we are not satisfied and we will not be satisfied until justice rolls down like waters and righteousness like a mighty stream.

Think Aloud

[1] *I have questions about the history of civil rights, but Dr. King gives examples of ways African Americans were treated unfairly in the United States. This helps me understand why he feels so strongly about demanding civil rights.*

. . . I say to you today, my friends, so even though we face the difficulties of today and tomorrow, I still have a dream. It is a dream deeply rooted in the American dream.

I have a dream that one day this nation will rise up and live out the true meaning of its creed: "We hold these truths to be self-evident, that all men are created equal."

I have a dream that one day on the red hills of Georgia, the sons of former slaves and the sons of former slave owners will be able to sit down together at the table of brotherhood.

I have a dream that one day even the state of Mississippi, a state sweltering with the heat of injustice, sweltering with the heat of oppression, will be transformed into an oasis of freedom and justice.

I have a dream that my four little children will one day live in a nation where they will not be judged by the color of their skin but by the content of their character. I have a dream today.

I have a dream that . . . one day right there in Alabama little black boys and black girls will be able to join hands with little white boys and white girls as sisters and brothers. I have a dream today. . . .

My country, 'tis of thee, sweet land of liberty, of thee I sing. Land where my fathers died, land of the pilgrim's pride, From every mountainside, let freedom ring!**²**

And if America is to be a great nation, this must become true. So let freedom ring from the <u>prodigious</u> hilltops of New Hampshire. Let freedom ring from the mighty mountains of New York. Let freedom ring from the heightening Alleghenies of Pennsylvania. Let freedom ring from the snow-capped Rockies of Colorado.

Let freedom ring from the curvaceous slopes of California. But not only that: Let freedom ring from Stone Mountain of Georgia. Let freedom ring from Lookout Mountain of Tennessee. Let freedom ring from every hill and molehill of Mississippi.**³**

From every mountainside, let freedom ring.

And when this happens, when we allow freedom ring, when we let it ring from every village and every hamlet, from every state and every city, we will be able to speed up that day when all of God's children, black men and white men, Jews and Gentiles, Protestants and Catholics, will be able to join hands and sing in the words of the old Negro spiritual: Free at last! Free at last! Thank God Almighty, we are free at last!

Genre Study

Persuasive Speech: The writer of a persuasive piece shares his or her opinions and may express them with great emotion and force. Dr. King feels strongly about the injustices he speaks about and he expresses great emotion as he describes his vision of true freedom and equality.

Think Aloud

²I can make a connection when Dr. King says to let freedom ring. These are the lyrics from the song "America the Beautiful." I think Dr. King includes the lyrics to show that even though we sing about America being a free country, this was not true for all people.

Think Aloud

³I wonder why Dr. King is mentioning so many states. He must be including them all in his dream.

After Reading

Take Notes: Have students discuss examples of word choice that Dr. King uses to achieve the purpose of his message. Ask students to revisit the purpose for reading and determine if the speech was meaningful and influenced the listeners.

Student Think Aloud

Use Copying Master number 1 to prompt students to share questions they may have about the speech and its origins.

"I wonder . . ."

Cultural Perspective

Rev. Dr. Martin Luther King, Jr., was influenced by the life and teachings of Mahatma Gandhi, who had spent much of his life trying to free the people of India from British rule. Dr. King went to India in 1959 and studied *satyagraha* (Sanskrit for "truth and firmness"), Gandhi's principle of peaceful persuasion. Discuss the relevance of ethnicity, culture, and history in relation to Gandhi and King's works.

Think and Respond

1. President Abraham Lincoln ended slavery with the Emancipation Proclamation. Why do you think Dr. King mentioned this decree at the beginning of his speech? *Possible response: He wanted to show that even though African Americans were freed from slavery 100 years ago, they were not truly free to live their lives.* **Inferential**

2. What phrases does Dr. King repeat in his speech? Why do you think he does this? *Possible responses: One hundred years later, we can never be satisfied, I have a dream, let freedom ring; I think he repeats these words because he wants people to remember what he is saying.* **Evaluate**

3. Why do you think it is important to read and think about Dr. King's speech? Why is his message still important to people today? *Possible response: We need to remember that freedom and rights need to be protected.* **Author's Purpose**

The Get Rich Quick Club

by Dan Gutman

Genre: Fiction

Comprehension Strategy: Monitor Comprehension

Think-Aloud Copying Master number 8

Before Reading

Genre: Tell students they will listen to a short excerpt, or section, from a novel. Remind them that a novel is a book about fictional or made-up characters and events. In this excerpt, the story is told from the point of view of the main character.

Expand Vocabulary: To help students better understand the selection, introduce the following words before reading:

flurries: bursts of light snow riding on gusts of wind

accumulation: something that gathers and piles up, such as snow

Microsoft®: the name of a well-known computer software company

vast: great in number, size, or extent; huge

Set a Purpose for Reading: Invite students to listen to find out who Gina is and how her dream relates to her main goal in life.

During Reading

Use the comprehension Think Alouds during the first reading of the story. The note about the genre may be used during subsequent readings.

THE GET RICH QUICK CLUB

by Dan Gutman

INTRODUCTION

It was a dream. I *think* it was a dream, anyway.

I'm just lying out there in the backyard one night, staring up at the sky. Then suddenly a dollar bill lands on my face. I pick it up. It looks real. I have no idea where it came from.

Then another one falls. And another. I look up and see bills fluttering down from the clouds above me. First they come in flurries, and then it turns into a snowstorm of money.

Tens. Twenties. Fifties. Hundreds. They're raining down on me, and *only* on me. It's more money than I could ever imagine. I am incredibly rich. I can buy anything in the world.

The money is piling up high. I grab handfuls of bills and throw them into the air for the fun of it. There's a foot of accumulation on the ground now. I take a running jump into it, like I'm jumping into a pile of October leaves.

Then a blinding flash of white light illuminates the sky.[1] It's so bright, I have to close my eyes. But I can still see the light through my eyelids. It hurts. I scream.

"Gina! Gina!" It's my mother's voice. "Gina, are you okay?"

I open my eyes. I'm in my bedroom now. No light. No money. I get up and rush to the window, half expecting to see the backyard covered in bills.

But there's nothing there. I guess it was just a dream.

NOTHING TO BE ASHAMED OF

I, Gina Tumolo, love money. So I guess it makes sense for me to dream about it.

I, Gina Tumolo, want to be a millionaire.[2]

There, I said it. I know it's not cool to say it, but it's the truth, so I might as well admit it.

Genre Study

Novel Excerpt: In this selection, the narrator is the main character, Gina. Words like *I*, *me*, and *my* indicate this feature of the text.

Think Aloud

[1] *I am not sure what illuminates means, but I can reread the text around it to help me figure out its meaning. It says there is a flash of light and the light is blinding. Something that blinds your eyes is very bright. The speaker's dream takes place at night, so I think* illuminates *means "to light up."*

Think Aloud

[2] *I figured out Gina was dreaming about money falling from the sky because money is very important to her.*

Ever since I was a little girl, I have loved money. In fact, the first memory I have is of money. I was sitting on the couch watching TV one day, and I found a dollar bill stuck inside the cushions. I must have been four years old.

I remember looking at those mysterious markings on the bill. The pyramid with that creepy-looking eye floating through it. What did it mean, I wondered? It all seemed very mystical and magical and wonderful.

I realize that money is just pieces of paper and disks of metal. But from a very young age, I was aware that those papers and disks were powerful. They could be exchanged for *other* things. You could turn them into just about *anything*.

This was amazing to me. You could actually walk into a store, hand somebody some green pieces of paper, and then take something from the store to bring home with you. To keep!

Incredible! And the more of that green paper you had, I quickly learned, the more stuff you could bring home.

Wow! What a fantastic idea! I wanted to get as much of that green paper as possible.

I never had many toys when I was little. My parents didn't have much money back then. Whenever I asked for something, they would give me the old line "It costs too much," or "Money doesn't grow on trees." Maybe that's why all I ever wanted was to accumulate as much money as I could.[3]

We learned in school that King Tut became the ruler of all Egypt when he was about my age, eleven. He owned all the treasures of the kingdom. Bill Gates, I know, started <u>Microsoft</u> when he was barely twenty, and it wasn't long before he became the richest person in the world.

Why not me? I asked myself. Why can't I, Gina Tumolo, accumulate a <u>vast</u> fortune at a very young age? What's stopping me?

Nothing. Other kids want to be in the Olympics, or they want to become rock stars or presidents. Good for them. I want to be a millionaire. My goal is to make my first million before I'm a teenager.

Think Aloud

[3] *I think this part is important because it helps me understand why money is so important to Gina. She says she did not have many toys when she was young because her parents did not have a lot of money.*

After Reading

Retell the Story: Have students illustrate two scenes from the story: one from Gina's early childhood and one of her as a teenage millionaire. For the second picture, ask students to predict a way Gina might have earned a million dollars. Invite students to discuss how the two pictures are related.

Student Think Aloud

Use Copying Master number 8 to prompt students to discuss parts of the story that required rereading or reading ahead for comprehension.

> "When I read _____, I had to reread, read back, read on . . ."

Think and Respond

1. Why does Gina say money is "powerful"? *Possible response: She feels anyone can use money to get the things they want at the store.* **Analytical**

2. Do you think this excerpt comes from the beginning, middle, or end of the novel *The Get Rich Quick Club*? Why? *Possible response: I think it comes from the beginning because we learn only about the main character and not what happens to her.* **Genre**

3. Given what the author has told us about Gina, do you think it is possible that she will become a teenage millionaire? *Accept reasonable responses. Possible responses: Yes, it is possible because she has set her mind on a goal and she will work toward it. No, it is not possible because she is too young to have a job that would pay her that much money.* **Author's Purpose**

Old Crow Warriors

by Frederick M. Howe III, age 17, Crow Nation

Genre: Poetry

Poetic Element: Imagery

Comprehension Strategy: Monitor Comprehension

Think-Aloud Copying Master number 8

Before Reading

Genre: Tell students they will listen to a poem written by a 17-year-old poet from the Crow nation. Remind them that unlike writers of fiction, poets have a small amount of space in which to describe their subject and express their message. In a short poem like this one, readers should carefully consider each word and what it contributes to the poem.

Expand Vocabulary: To help students better understand the poem, introduce the following words before reading it:

> *swaying:* moving from side to side

> *crisp:* fresh, invigorating

Set a Purpose for Reading: For the first reading, have students listen and enjoy the language. Invite them to visualize an image based on the words used by the poet.

During Reading

To emphasize the rhetorical questions, lift your voice at the end of each question. Read through the poem the first time without interruptions. Then reread, pausing to draw students' attention to the comprehension Think Aloud and genre note.

Old Crow Warriors

by Frederick M. Howe III

Watching the trees <u>swaying</u>,

the beautiful colors of leaves.

Take a breath. Can you feel

the <u>crisp</u> cold air enter

your lungs?

Look, look, the gray cloud.

Is there no end?

Winter is upon us.

Shhh. Hear that?

The voices, the voices

of old Crow warriors.[1]

Hear them? They're telling

me to be strong.

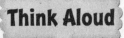

Think Aloud

[1] *I wonder what the voices are saying. The speaker says they are the voices of Crow warriors who lived long ago. When I reread, I realize that he hears them in nature. He worries that winter will never end, and they give him hope by telling him to be strong.*

After Reading

Set a Purpose for Rereading: Reread the poem for the purpose of exploring its imagery and deeper meanings with students.

Student Think Aloud

Use Copying Master number 8 to prompt students to share how rereading answered questions they had about the poem.

"When I read _____, I had to reread, read back, read on . . ."

Cultural Perspective

There were several ways Crow men could prove that they were true warriors. They could show bravery and leadership in battle. They could lead a successful war party. Men who captured an enemy's horse or weapon during battle were especially honored. Discuss bravery as a theme in literature across cultures and times.

Think and Respond

1. Why do you think the poet includes questions in his poem? *Possible responses: They make it seem like the boy is speaking directly to the reader. This makes me feel like I am a part of the poem or that I am there with the boy.* **Inferential**

2. What might the poet be hinting at when he uses the image of the gray clouds? *Possible response: The poet might be referring to dark, or negative, thoughts hanging over his head. So there is no end in sight to the poet's troubles.* **Poetic Element**

3. The poet says the voices of the old Crow warriors are telling him to be strong. Why do you think the poet included this in the poem? *Accept reasonable responses. Possible response: The poet probably finds courage in his ancestors' words. The poet may be encouraging us to do the same.* **Author's Purpose**

Water Dance

by Thomas Locker

Genre: Poetry

Poetic Element: Personification

Comprehension Strategy: Visualize

Think-Aloud Copying Master number 3

Before Reading

Genre: Tell students they will read a free-verse poem. Remind them that free verse does not have a regular pattern of rhyming words or line lengths. However, students may be able to find other types of patterns in the poem.

Expand Vocabulary: To help students capture the imagery of this poem, introduce the following words before reading:

> *cascade:* to fall in a tumbling motion
>
> *wind:* to move along in a curving path
>
> *palisades:* cliffs
>
> *drench:* to cover or soak with water

Set a Purpose for Reading: For the first reading, have students listen to find out who is speaking in the poem and to enjoy the descriptions of the many different forms water takes.

During Reading

Emphasize the repetition of the lines in italic by reading them with the same tone or expression. Read through the poem the first time without interruptions. Then reread, pausing to draw students' attention to the comprehension Think Aloud and genre note.

Water Dance

by Thomas Locker

Some people say that I am one thing.
Others say that I am many.
Ever since the world began
I have been moving in an endless circle.
Sometimes I fall from the sky.

I am the rain.

Sometimes I cascade.
I tumble
down,
down,
over the moss-covered rocks,
through the forest shadows.

I am the mountain stream.

At the foot of the mountains,
I leap from a stone cliff.
Spiraling.
Plunging.

I am the waterfall.[1]

In the shadows of the mountain,
I am still and deep.
I fill
and overflow.

I am the lake.

I wind through broad, golden valleys
joined by streams,
joined by creeks.
I grow ever wider,
broader and deeper.

I am the river.

I pass through a gateway
of high stone palisades,
leaving the land behind.
Cool silver moonlight
sparkles and dances
on my waves.

Think Aloud

[1]*I read and reread each stanza to understand that the poem is like a riddle. First the poet describes a form of water, then he reveals its name in the final line.*

I am the sea.

Drawn upward
by warm sunlight,
in white-silver veils
I rise into the air.
I disappear.

I am the mist.

In thousands of shapes I reappear
high above the earth in the blue sky.
I float.
I drift.

I am the clouds.

Carried by winds
from distant seas
I move,
growing heavier,
growing darker,
returning.

I am the storm front.

At the wall of the mountains,
I rise up
as gleaming power-filled towers
in the darkened sky.

I am the thunderhead.

I blind the sky with lightning.
The earth trembles with my thunder.
I rage.
I drench the mountainside.

I am the storm.

Storms come.
Storms pass.
I am countless droplets of rain
left floating in the silent air.
I reflect all the colors of sunlight.

I am the rainbow.

I am one thing.
I am many things.

I am water.

This is my dance through our world.

Genre Study

Poetry: In some poems, a nonliving thing is personified, or given human qualities. In this poem, water is describing itself, just as a person would.

Set a Purpose for Rereading: Reread the poem for the purpose of having students trace the water cycle. Ask them to summarize the ways in which the poet describes each form of water.

Student Think Aloud

Use Copying Master number 3 to prompt students to share how the images and descriptions in the poem helped them to visualize the forms of water.

"I was able to picture in my mind . . ."

Cultural Perspective

The world's longest river is the Nile in Africa. Its length is listed at 4,160 miles (6,695 km). The world's highest waterfall is the Salto Angel in Venezuela. It has a total drop of 3,212 feet (979 m).

Think and Respond

1. What do you think the words "I am one thing/I am many things" mean? *Possible responses: It means water can be just water, and it can also take different forms. Some people see water as one thing while others see it as many things.* **Inferential**

2. How does the poet's choice of the pronoun "I" in the poem affect the discussion of the water cycle? *Possible response: The poem starts with water falling from the sky as rain. The next part describes different forms of water on the land. The last part shows water returning to the sky as clouds and storms. Throughout the water cycle, though, water is telling the story.* **Poetic Element**

3. What do you think the author's purpose was for writing the poem? *Possible responses: He wanted to entertain and inform.* **Author's Purpose**

HACHIKO:
The True Story of a Loyal Dog
by Pamela S. Turner

Genre: Narrative Nonfiction

Comprehension Strategy: Visualize

Think-Aloud Copying Master number 3

Before Reading

Genre: Tell students you will read aloud a narrative nonfiction selection. Remind them that this type of selection tells a true story about an event. Explain that the setting of the story is a train station in Tokyo, Japan.

Expand Vocabulary: Introduce the following words before reading:

> *kimonos:* a loose robe that is tied with a sash
>
> *strode:* walked confidently
>
> *timidly:* shyly
>
> *morsel:* a very small piece of food

Set a Purpose for Reading: Invite students to listen to find out why and how Hachiko was a loyal dog.

During Reading

Use the comprehension Think Alouds during the first reading of the story. Notes about the genre and cultural perspective may be used during subsequent readings.

HACHIKO: The True Story of a Loyal Dog

by Pamela S. Turner

There is a statue of my old friend at the entrance to Shibuya Station. His bronze feet are bright and shiny, polished by thousands of friendly hands. There is a sign that says, simply, "Loyal dog Hachiko." I close my eyes and remember the day we met, so long ago.

When I was six years old, my family moved to a little house in Tokyo near the Shibuya train station. At first the trains frightened me. But after a while, I grew to enjoy their power and the furious noises they made. One day I begged Mama to take me to meet Papa as he came home on the afternoon train. She laughed and said, "Kentaro, you have become big and brave, just like a samurai!" Together we walked to the station.

It was spring, and the day was clear and cold. There were tiny carts all around the station, selling snacks, newspapers, and hundreds of other things to the crowds of people rushing by. Ladies in <u>kimonos</u> walked carefully, trying to keep their white tabi socks away from the grime of the streets. Businessmen <u>strode</u> about, hurrying home or to catch another train. Mama and I had stopped near the station entrance when I noticed the dog.[1]

He was sitting quietly, all alone, by a newspaper stand. He had thick, cream-colored fur, small pointed ears, and a broad, bushy tail that curved up over his back. I wondered if the dog was a stray, but he was wearing a nice leather harness and looked healthy and strong.

His brown eyes were fixed on the station entrance.

Just then, Papa appeared. He was chatting with an older man. The dog bounded over to the man, his entire body wiggling and quivering with delight. His eyes shone, and his mouth curled up into something that looked, to me, just like a smile.

"Ah, Kentaro! You see, Dr. Ueno, you are not the only one who has someone to welcome him," said Papa. He introduced us to the older man. "Dr. Ueno works with me at Tokyo Imperial University."

"What is your dog's name?" I asked <u>timidly</u>. The dog was beautiful, but his sharp face reminded me of a wolf's. I grabbed Mama's kimono and stepped behind her, just in case.

"Don't be afraid," said Dr. Ueno kindly. "This is Hachiko. He is big, but still a puppy. He walks me to the station every

Think Aloud

[1]*I wonder why the author started the story with a description of Hachiko's statue. She then recalled first meeting the dog in her childhood.*

morning and waits for me to come home every afternoon. I think Hachiko stores up all his joy, all day long, and then lets it out all at once!"

Hachiko stood wagging his tail next to Dr. Ueno. I reached out to touch him, and he bounced forward and sniffed my face. I yelped and jumped back behind Mama.

They all laughed. "Oh, Kentaro, don't worry—he just wants to get to know you," said Dr. Ueno. "Dogs can tell a lot about people just by smelling them. Why, Hachiko probably knows what you ate for lunch!"

I sniffed my hand, but it didn't smell like rice balls to me. I reached out and touched Hachiko gently on the shoulder. "His fur is so thick and soft," I said. "Like a bear's."

"Dogs like Hachiko once hunted bears in the north, where it is very cold and snowy," said Dr. Ueno, kneeling down next to me and rubbing Hachiko's ears.

From that day on, I went to the station almost every afternoon. But I no longer went to see the trains. I went to see Hachiko. He was always there, waiting near the newspaper stand. I often saved a morsel from my lunch and hid it in one of my pockets. Hachiko would sniff me all over, wagging his tail, until he found a sticky bit of fish or soybean cake. Then he would nudge me with his nose, as if to say, "Give me my prize!" When it was cold, I would bury my face in the thick ruff of creamy fur around his neck.

One day in May, I was waiting at the station with Hachiko. The moment I saw Papa, I knew something was wrong. He was alone, and he walked hunched over, staring sadly at the gray pavement under his feet.[2] "What's the matter, Papa?" I asked him anxiously, standing with one hand on Hachiko's broad head.

He sighed. "Kentaro, let's go home." Hachiko's bright brown eyes followed us as we walked away, but he stayed behind, waiting for Dr. Ueno.

When we got home, Papa told us that Dr. Ueno had died that morning at the university. I was stunned. "But what will happen to Hachiko?" I asked, blinking hard to keep the tears back. "What will he do?"

"I don't know," said Papa. "Perhaps Dr. Ueno's relatives will take him in."

"What about tonight?" I asked. "Can we go see if he is all right?"

Think Aloud

[2] I think something bad has happened. I can visualize Kentaro's father from the description of how he walks. He seems to be upset because he is staring at the ground and he is hunched over. He is also alone, so he may be sad that Dr. Ueno is not there.

Papa was very sad and tired, but he walked with me back to Shibuya Station. Hachiko was curled up by the newspaper stand. He wagged his tail when he saw us. Papa and I gave him water in an old chipped bowl and some food. Hachiko ate and drank, but he kept looking up toward the station entrance for Dr. Ueno. Papa and I left even sadder than we had come.

The next day, I went back to check on Hachiko, but he was not there. Papa told me that Hachiko had been taken several miles away to live with some of Dr. Ueno's relatives. "But I'll never see him again!" I cried. "Why can't he live with us?"

"We don't have room for a dog," protested Papa. "And Hachiko really belongs to Dr. Ueno's relatives, now that Dr. Ueno is dead. Hachiko is better off having a home than sitting at a train station."

But Hachiko had other ideas. A few days later he was back at Shibuya Station, patiently waiting, his brown eyes fixed on the entrance. Hachiko had run back to his old home, and from there to Shibuya Station.[3]

Mama and Papa let me take food and water to Hachiko every day. Mama grumbled a bit about the food, saying we couldn't afford to feed a big bear like Hachiko, but she always seemed to cook more rice than we could eat.

Think Aloud

[3]I know now why Hachiko is called "a loyal dog" in this story's title. He traveled several miles to the train station to wait for Dr. Ueno. This information helps me make this connection.

Other people at the station took an interest in Hachiko. Men and women who rode Papa and Dr. Ueno's train stopped by to scratch his ears and say a few kind words. One day I saw an old man filling Hachiko's water bowl as Hachiko licked his hand. The old man's hair was streaked with gray, and he was stooped, as if he had spent most of his life bent over the ground. But his eyes were as sharp and bright as Hachiko's.

"Are you young Kentaro?" the old man asked. I nodded. "I'm Mr. Kobayashi. I was Dr. Ueno's gardener. Dr. Ueno told me that you and Hachiko often wait for the afternoon train together."

"Do you still take care of the house where Dr. Ueno lived?" I asked.

"Yes," said Mr. Kobayashi. "Hachiko comes back to the house every night to sleep on the porch. But in the morning, he walks to the station just like he did with Dr. Ueno. When the last train leaves the station, he returns home."

We were both silent. Then I asked, "Do you think Hachiko knows that Dr. Ueno died?"

Think Aloud

[4] *Now I understand the significance of the statue at the beginning and at the end of the story. The memorial of Hachiko is just as important as his story.*

Mr. Kobayashi said thoughtfully, "I don't know, Kentaro. Perhaps he still hopes that Dr. Ueno will return someday. Or perhaps he knows Dr. Ueno is dead, but he waits at the station to honor his master's memory."

As the years passed and Hachiko got older, he became very stiff and could barely walk to Shibuya Station. But still he went, every day. People began collecting money to build a statue of Hachiko at the station. Papa, Mama, and I all gave money, and we were very happy when the statue was placed next to the spot Hachiko had waited for so many years.

One chilly morning I woke to the sound of Mama crying. "What's wrong?" I asked as I stumbled into the kitchen. Papa sat silently at the table, and Mama turned her tear-stained face to me. "Hachiko died last night at Shibuya Station," she choked. "Still waiting for Dr. Ueno."

I was seventeen, and too big to cry. But I went into the other room and did not come out for a long time.

Later that day we all went to the station. To our great surprise, Hachiko's spot near the newspaper stand was covered in flowers placed there by his many friends.

Old Mr. Kobayashi was there. He shuffled over to me and put a hand on my shoulder.

"Hachiko didn't come back to the house last night," he said quietly. "I walked to the station and found him. I think his spirit is with Dr. Ueno's, don't you?"

"Yes," I whispered.

The big bronze statue of Hachiko is a very famous meeting place. Shibuya Station is enormous now, and hundreds of thousands of people travel through it every day. People always say to each other, "Let's meet at Hachiko." Today Hachiko is a place where friends and family long separated come together again.[4]

 **After Reading**

Retell the Story: Have students discuss the events of the story and share their responses to it. Students should use the opinions and reactions of the teacher as well as classmates to evaluate their personal interpretation of ideas, information, and experiences.

Student Think Aloud

Use Copying Master 3 to prompt students to discuss which scenes they were able to visualize most easily and why.

"I was able to picture in my mind . . ."

Cultural Perspective

Discuss the cultural elements of the story: the setting, the formal way in which people greet each other. Then explain that Hachiko's real name was Hachi. But people who came to see the dog added "ko" to the end of his name as a nickname. "Ko" means "child" in Japanese.

Think and Respond

1. Why do you think so many people donated money to help build a statue of Hachiko? *Possible responses: People admired Hachiko for showing loyalty to his owner for so many years and they wanted to honor him. People probably thought of Hachiko as their own dog because they saw him every day when they went to work.* **Inferential**

2. The events of the narrative are presented in the order in which they happened. Identify some examples of words and phrases the author uses to show sequence. *Possible responses: When I was six years old; It was spring; One day in May; When we got home; The next day; As the years passed and Hachiko got older; I was seventeen; Later that day* **Genre**

3. Why do you think Pamela S. Turner chose to write about Hachiko? *Possible responses: The story of Hachiko is true, interesting, and unique. She knew many people own and love dogs and would enjoy reading a story about a dog.* **Author's Purpose**

WILLIAM "DUMMY" HOY: Baseball's Silent Hero

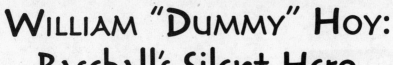

by Constance Keremes

Genre: Biography

Comprehension Strategy: Generate Questions

Think-Aloud Copying Master number 1

Before Reading

Genre: Explain to students that they will hear a biography of a man who made an important contribution to the sport of baseball. Remind students that a biography presents facts and interesting details about a person's life. The subject of a biography is usually someone who has done something noteworthy or unique.

Expand Vocabulary: Introduce the following words before reading:

> *cobbler:* someone who repairs shoes
>
> *feat:* an unusual act, usually based on skill
>
> *horse and buggy carriage:* a horse-drawn vehicle
>
> *en masse:* as a whole group

Set a Purpose for Reading: Invite students to listen to find out why William Hoy is called baseball's "silent hero."

During Reading

Use the comprehension Think Alouds during the first reading of the story. Notes about the genre and cultural perspective may be used during subsequent readings.

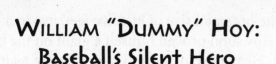

WILLIAM "DUMMY" HOY:
Baseball's Silent Hero

by Constance Keremes

Thwack! The sweetest sound a baseball player ever hears is the crack of bat against ball. William "Dummy" Hoy never heard that special sound, though he was one of the greatest ball players in baseball history.

William Hoy was born on May 23, 1862 in Houcktown, Ohio. When he was just two years old, he became very sick with meningitis, a serious illness that left him deaf.

Although William could no longer hear, he still managed to learn how to play baseball. He never missed a chance to toss around a ball, often taking time off from the <u>cobbler</u> shop where he worked to play catch with the neighborhood children. He became an excellent player. One day someone noticed how well he played, and suggested that he join a baseball game in another town.

Soon William Hoy was on his way to a professional baseball career. In 1886, when he was 24 years old, he began playing in Oshkosh, Wisconsin. Back in those early days of baseball, over a hundred years ago, umpires shouted their calls during games. William's deafness made it impossible to hear such calls. After every pitch, he would have to ask his coach if the umpire had called a ball or strike. Often, the pitcher on the other team would unfairly "quick-pitch" William as he spoke with his coach, throwing another ball before William was ready for it.

In 1887, William came up with an idea to make the game fairer. He asked the third-base coach to use hand signals to tell what the pitch was called. William adapted signals he had learned from American Sign Language. "The coach at third kept me posted by lifting his right hand for strikes and his left for balls," William explained. Now William did not have to waste time conferring with his coach when he was up at bat.[1]

"That gave umpires an idea," William bragged. Soon umpires started using hand signals, too. William Hoy's signals are still used in baseball games today. Those two simple signals in fact led to many other important ones now used by umpires, managers, and outfielders in both baseball and softball.

Think Aloud

[1] *I wonder if this idea to use hand signals grew to become part of baseball and other sports today. I will read on to find out why it was important.*

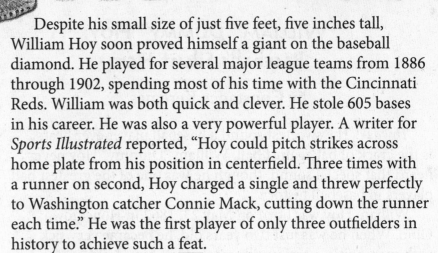

Despite his small size of just five feet, five inches tall, William Hoy soon proved himself a giant on the baseball diamond. He played for several major league teams from 1886 through 1902, spending most of his time with the Cincinnati Reds. William was both quick and clever. He stole 605 bases in his career. He was also a very powerful player. A writer for *Sports Illustrated* reported, "Hoy could pitch strikes across home plate from his position in centerfield. Three times with a runner on second, Hoy charged a single and threw perfectly to Washington catcher Connie Mack, cutting down the runner each time." He was the first player of only three outfielders in history to achieve such a <u>feat</u>.

Nothing could stop William from making a play. He is said to have chased after a fly ball, leaping up on a <u>horse and buggy carriage</u> to make a catch. Legend has it that he even mounted the horse.

William Hoy taught his teammates how to communicate. Sam Crawford, who played with William in the outfield, explained, "I'd be in right field and he'd be in center, and I'd have to listen real careful to know whether or not he'd take a fly ball. He'd make a kind of throaty noise, kind of a little squawk, and when a fly ball came out and I heard this little noise I knew he was going to take it. We never had any trouble about who was to take the ball."

They called him "Dummy." The nickname sounds cruel today, but many years ago people who could not hear or speak were often called deaf and dumb. William said that his nickname never bothered him. He probably knew that his teammates respected the great job he did on the field. Those teammates also admired his politeness. William was never sent out of a game for misconduct.[2]

William also brought a sense of honesty and fairness to the sport of baseball. One day an umpire called a batter out after a ball seemed to be caught on the fly. Because it was dark, both teams argued over the call. Even though the other team would benefit, William, who had seen the play, honestly reported that the ball was caught before it bounced.

William's fans admired him, too. In 1892, a writer for *Sporting Life* wrote, "When outfielder Hoy made a brilliant catch, the crowd arose '<u>en masse</u>' and wildly waved hats and arms." It was a

silent cheer that they knew William would understand. William Hoy proved himself equally outstanding a man off the baseball diamond. He always enjoyed working with children. After retiring from baseball in 1903, he devoted much time to working with the hearing-impaired community near his home in Ohio. He served as Goodyear's personnel director to deaf workers. William also found time to coach the Goodyear Silents baseball club, a team of hearing-impaired players.

In 1951, William Hoy became the first player to be enshrined in the American Athletic Association of the Deaf's Hall of Fame. Always active, even in his old age, William threw out the first ball at Opening Day of the World Series in October 1961. He died just two months later, at 99 years of age.

Although over forty years have passed since William Hoy died, his legend lives on in both the baseball world and the hearing-impaired community. Athletes of all abilities and physical challenges can find in William Hoy the inspiration to make their own dreams come true.[3]

Think Aloud

[3]*This helps me understand why the author chose to write about William Hoy. She thinks that other people might be inspired to follow their dreams after reading about all of the things Hoy accomplished.*

Retell the story: Have students summarize the important events from William Hoy's life.

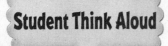
Student Think Aloud

Use Copying Master 1 to prompt students to share questions they had while reading the selection.

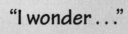
"I wonder . . ."

Cultural Perspective

Discuss with students the historical significance of Hoy's achievements in sports. Talk about how Hoy's system may have changed other sports. Since 1924, athletes have been competing in the World Games for the Deaf, now known as the Deaflympics. Just under two hundred athletes competed in the first competition, which was the idea of Eugène Rubens-Alcais of France. Today thousands of deaf and hearing-impaired athletes compete for their countries.

Think and Respond

1. How does the author show that Hoy was a hero off the baseball field as well as on it? *Possible responses: She says that he worked with other hearing-impaired people. He coached a baseball team of hearing-impaired players.* **Analytical**

2. How does the author add interest to the selection? *Possible responses: She includes quotations from other players and people who watched William Hoy play. She tells about specific things that happened during games.* **Genre**

3. The author calls William Hoy a "silent hero." Do you think it is appropriate for the author to describe him as a hero? Why or why not? *Accept reasonable responses. Possible responses: Yes, because a hero is a person who shows exceptional courage or strength, just like Hoy did when he chose to play in spite of his hearing impairment.* **Author's Purpose**

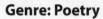

At the Flick of a Switch

by Pat Moon

Genre: Poetry

Poetic Elements: Rhyme, Onomatopoeia

Comprehension Strategy: Generate Questions

Think-Aloud Copying Master number 1

Before Reading

Genre: Remind students that a rhyming poem contains a rhyming pattern. Rhyming words may be used at the end of each line, every other line, or sometimes in a more complex pattern. Point out that this particular poem also contains sound words, a poetic element known as onomatopoeia. Writers use such words to emphasize the sound that something makes. It also adds a musical quality to the writing.

Expand Vocabulary: To help students understand the poem, which was written in the early 1980s, introduce the following words:

> *percolator:* a type of coffee machine that forces water through the ground coffee
>
> *liquidizer:* a type of blender or food processor
>
> *deep-fat fryer:* a container or pot that fries food in oil at high temperatures

Set a Purpose for Reading: Have students listen for how the poet feels about the use of all these appliances.

During Reading

To emphasize the sound words, use an expressive tone. Read through the poem the first time without interruptions. Then reread, pausing to draw students' attention to the comprehension Think Aloud and genre note.

At the Flick of a Switch

by Pat Moon

Swish goes the washing machine,
Grrrr goes the grater,

Ping goes the microwave,
Pdpp the <u>percolator</u>,

Brmmmm goes the vacuum cleaner,
Whim, the tumble dryer,

Wizzz goes the <u>liquidizer</u>,
Sizzz, the <u>deep-fat fryer</u>.[1]

There goes the thingy-me-bob
That makes the fizzy drinks,

With all the other thingy-me-bobs
To the cupboard under the sink.

Up go more power stations,
Up goes the smoke,

Cough-cough goes this planet,
"You're going to make me choke."

Think Aloud

[1] *I was able to picture in my mind the different appliances because the poet begins each line with a sound word and then names the appliance that makes the sound. I wonder if the poet feels that having so many appliances is a good thing or a bad thing.*

After Reading

Set a Purpose for Rereading: Reread the poem for the purpose of exploring its deeper meanings, including the poet's message. Emphasize the last four lines. Have students write their own poem using rhyme and the sounds of language.

Student Think Aloud

Use Copying Master number 1 to prompt students to share questions they had about the poet's word choice or the images in the poem.

"I wonder . . ."

Think and Respond

1. How do the last four lines contrast with the rest of the poem? *Possible responses: The first part is all about the appliances and the last part is about how these appliances affect Earth. The first part takes place in a kitchen and the last part shows what is happening in the world.* **Analytical**

2. Think about the different patterns in the poem. Identify some. *Possible responses: rhyming words, sound words, sound words are mentioned before the name of the appliance* **Genre**

3. What is the poet's purpose for writing this poem? What message do you think she wanted to share with her readers? *Possible response: She wants to show that the appliances in our homes add to the pollution on Earth because they use electricity or some other energy in order to work.* **Author's Purpose**

Whale in the Sky
by Anne Siberell

Genre: Legend

Comprehension Strategy: Visualize

Think-Aloud Copying Master number 3

Before Reading

Genre: Tell students they will listen to a legend in which all of the main characters are animals. Remind them that people created legends as a way to explain the world around them. All legends focus on a specific time and place. Explain that this legend comes from the Northwest Coast Indians.

Expand Vocabulary: Introduce the following words before reading:

> *thunderbird:* according to Native American myth, a bird that causes thunder and lightning
>
> *horizon:* the line where the earth and sky seem to meet
>
> *salmon:* a type of fish
>
> *talons:* a bird's claws

Set a Purpose for Reading: Have students listen to find out what the problem is and what the solution will be.

During Reading

Use the comprehension Think Alouds during the first reading of the story. Notes about the genre and cultural perspective may be used during subsequent readings.

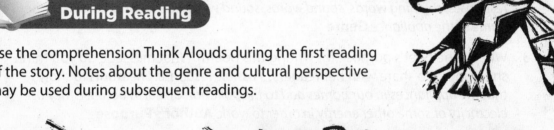

Whale in the Sky

by Anne Siberell

Long ago, the rivers and seas were filled with fish, and tall trees crowded the mountainsides. There was no written language among the Indian tribes of the Northwest, and storytellers passed history and legends from one generation to the next. Sometimes a chief would hire an artist to carve a story in pictures on the trunk of a giant tree. Whale in the Sky *is such a tale.*

The carved tree, called a totem pole, identified the chief and his family, his clan and tribe.[1]

In a time long ago, Thunderbird watched over the sea and land and all its creatures.

One day he saw Whale, small on the horizon of the sea. He did not see Frog, small on the bank of the river.

Frog trembled because Whale was growing larger. The salmon swam faster and faster as Whale chased them through the sea and into the river.[2]

Whale chased the salmon up the river and Frog was afraid. He called to Raven.

Raven flew into the sky after Thunderbird.

"Whale swallows the salmon and chases them into the river," he called.

Thunderbird stretched his great wings wide and flew like the wind.

He saw Whale in the river.

He grabbed Whale in his terrible talons and flew high up into the sky. Whale struggled and screamed.

Thunderbird flew higher and higher. Then he dropped Whale on the highest mountain.

Frog was safe. He thanked his friend Raven. Now there were salmon for the people who lived beside the river.

Whale gasped and shivered on the mountain. He promised to stay out of the river if he could return to the sea.[3]

Thunderbird clapped his great wings, and Whale slid down the mountain, back to the sea.

The chief of the people told this tale to the carver. The carver made the story into a totem pole.

Thunderbird holds Whale, while Raven watches over Salmon and Frog.

Think Aloud

[1] *Without written language, how do people pass on their culture and history? Indians of the Northwest told legends and created art such as totem poles that told stories.*

Think Aloud

[2] *I can picture the whale growing larger in my mind and understand why Frog was afraid.*

Think Aloud

[3] *I think Whale has learned a lesson. If he returns to the sea, he won't chase salmon into the rivers.*

Retell the Story: Have students retell the story. Ask students how frog solved his problem.

Student Think Aloud

Use Copying Master number 3 to prompt students to share which parts of the story they were able to visualize most easily.

"I was able to picture in my mind . . ."

Cultural Perspective

Greek and Scandinavian people passed down their history through legends and art just like the Indians of the Northwest Coast. Totem poles were an important part of life for Northwest Coast Indians. When a totem pole was raised, it was cause for great celebration. As part of the ceremony, hundreds of people would attend. The family or village responsible for the pole also fed all the visitors and handed out gifts.

Think and Respond

1. How are Thunderbird and the chief alike? *Possible responses: The chief and Thunderbird both look out for the people or animals below them.* **Analytical**

2. How can you tell that this story is a legend? *Possible responses: It has animals with human traits. It involves something that could not have happened in real life.* **Genre**

3. Why do you think the chief told this story to his people? *Possible responses: The chief told this story to his people to remind them about how he will protect them and solve their problems.* **Author's Purpose**

Long Trip

by Langston Hughes

Genre: Poetry

Poetic Element: Figurative Language

Comprehension Strategy: Visualize

Think-Aloud Copying Master number 3

Before Reading

Genre: Tell students they will listen to a poem that includes figurative language. Remind them that a metaphor is a direct comparison between two things. Give several examples, such as *This bedroom is a disaster zone* or *This class is a bee's nest of activity*.

Expand Vocabulary: Introduce the following words before reading to improve students' comprehension of the poem:

> *wilderness:* an area where everything is wild
>
> *dip:* to drop down
>
> *rise:* to go up

Set a Purpose for Reading: Have students listen for how the poet feels about the sea and to enjoy the language.

During Reading

Read slowly so students have a chance to think carefully about every word in this short poem. Read through the poem the first time without interruptions. Then reread, pausing to draw students' attention to the comprehension Think Aloud and genre note.

Long Trip

by Langston Hughes

The sea is a wilderness of waves,
A desert of water.
We dip and dive,
Rise and roll.
Hide and are hidden
On the sea.
  Day, night,
  Night, day,
The sea is a desert of waves,
A wilderness of water.[1]

Genre Study

Poetry: The poet uses metaphors in the first two lines to describe the sea as both a wilderness and a desert.

Think Aloud

[1] *I notice that there are a lot of repetitive sounds —* w, d, r, *and* h. *I was able to picture the repeated movements of the ocean in my mind because of the repeated sounds.*

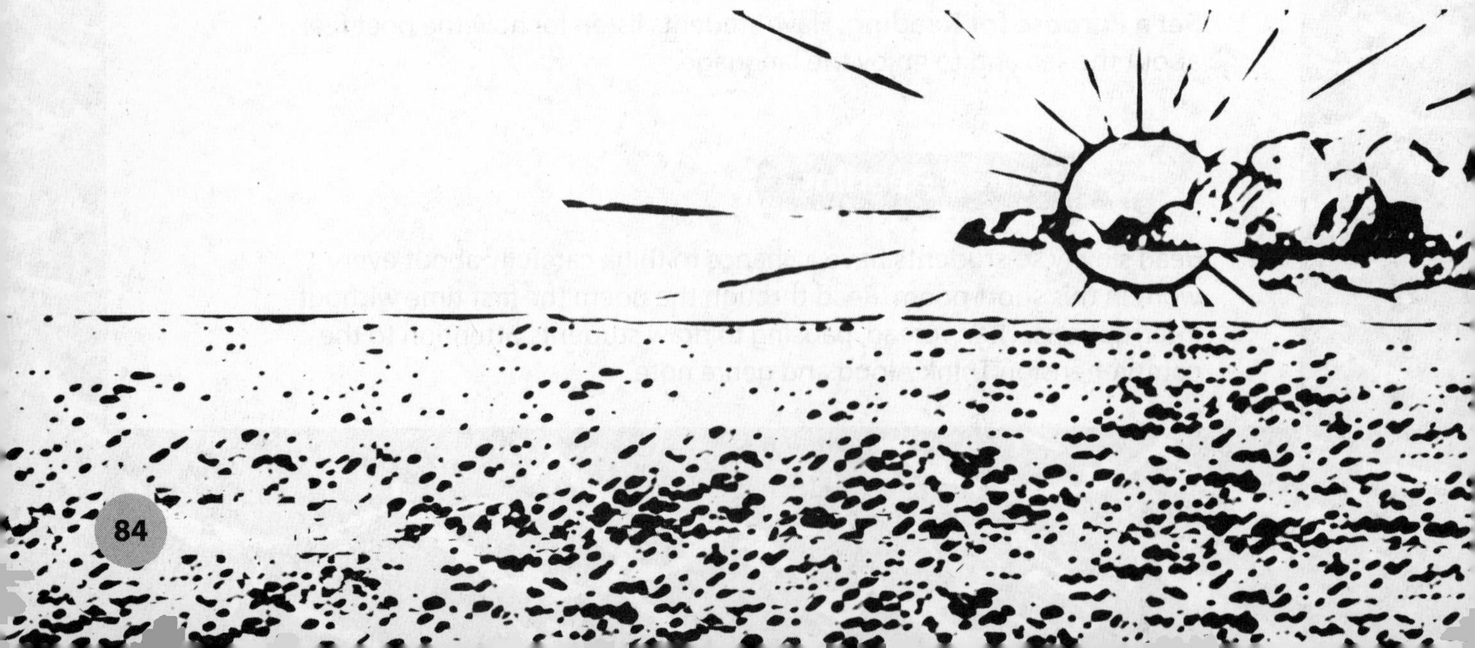

 **After Reading**

Set a Purpose for Rereading: Reread the poem for the purpose of having students explore its deeper meanings and the poet's use of metaphor and contrast. Explain that contrast is using opposites to describe something, such as dark and light.

Student Think Aloud

Use Copying Master number 3 to prompt students to discuss a line, image, or word choice that helped them visualize the poem.

"I was able to picture in my mind..."

Cultural Perspective

Langston Hughes, a prominent African American poet, worked as a seaman while traveling to Africa and Europe. He is known for his images of African American life during the 1920s through the 1960s.

Think and Respond

1. At what time is the sea like a wilderness? When might it be like a desert?
   Possible responses: The sea is like a wilderness when there are lots of waves and the water is moving up and down. The sea is like a desert when there are no waves and the water is totally flat. **Analytical**

2. The poem includes several examples of contrast. Identify some of them.
   Possible responses: day and night; dipping down and rising up on the waves; Sometimes the sea is wild and wavy and sometimes it is calm and flat; The sea (a wet place) is described as a desert (a place with little or no water). **Figurative Language**

3. The title of the poem is "Long Trip." Why do you think the poet chose this title?
   Accept reasonable responses. Possible responses: Perhaps the poet was inspired to write this poem after a boat trip. Perhaps it was a long trip where they saw nothing but water for days. **Author's Purpose**

READING AND RIDING

by Kathi Appelt and Jeanne Cannella Schmitzer

Genre: Historical Fiction

Comprehension Strategy: Summarize

Think-Aloud Copying Master number 7

 Before Reading

Genre: Tell students you will read aloud a realistic fiction selection about a group of traveling librarians. Explain that this type of text combines made-up characters with events that really happened. Tell students they should listen carefully to identify which elements of the text are fictional and which are true.

Expand Vocabulary: Introduce the following words to help students better understand the selection:

stoop: a step or group of steps outside a door

crooks and hollows: small, hard-to-reach areas

pamphlets: newsletters or short informational texts

constant: keeps happening; ongoing

Set a Purpose for Reading: Invite students to listen for the factual information about the Kentucky Pack Horse Library Project.

 **During Reading**

Use the comprehension Think Alouds during the first reading of the story. Notes about the genre and cultural perspective may be used during subsequent readings.

READING AND RIDING

by Kathi Appelt and Jeanne Cannella Schmitzer

It was a cold, gray morning in January of 1936. Slowly, a woman on horseback made her way across the stony hillsides of Kentucky. Freezing rain stung her face and soaked her thin coat.

At last, she reached her destination: a one-room schoolhouse nestled between two rocky peaks. Before she got to the stoop, the door burst open and a boy with sparkling eyes and a chipped front tooth grinned at her.

"We been a-waitin' for you, book lady," he said.

The woman smiled. As a librarian with Kentucky's Pack Horse Library Project, she was just doing her job: delivering books, on horseback, to people in the crooks and hollows of eastern Kentucky's mountains.[1]

The Kentucky Pack Horse Library Project began in 1935, during the dark years of the Great Depression. Many people in Kentucky, like millions of people across the United States, lost their jobs. There was not enough money for essentials like food, clothing, and medicine. Families lost their homes, and children went hungry. In such hard times, how could people get books?

The answer was the Kentucky Pack Horse Library Project. The way it worked was simple: The government of President Franklin D. Roosevelt paid women in rural Kentucky to carry books, magazines, and pamphlets to the poor homes and schools scattered throughout the Kentucky mountains. The librarians traveled on horseback because there were no paved or even gravel roads in the mountains.

Genre Study

Historical Fiction: The first three paragraphs provide a fictional introduction for the nonfictional information that is provided later. This type of information gives readers a better understanding of what it must have been like to deliver and receive books during that historical period.

Think Aloud

[1]*At first I thought the "book lady" was the boy's teacher and then I found out that she is really a librarian. She is bringing books to the school, so I guess she could be called a traveling librarian.*

Think Aloud

[2]I think these librarians had a tough and dangerous job. The women traveled alone. They had to cross fast-moving creeks and icy mountain routes. They must have believed strongly in the project to take on such a hard job.

Think Aloud

[3]I think this part is important because the author explains the impact of the pack horse library project. The people lived far away from cities. There were no televisions and possibly no radios either. Finding an actual quote from a pack horse librarian in the selection reminds me that these events really happened.

The life of a pack horse librarian was tough. The women traveled roughly eighteen miles a day, over the rockiest terrain, through all kinds of weather. All alone, they crossed dangerous creeks and climbed icy slopes.[2] Many people were suspicious of "book learnin'," and the librarians had to win their trust. Finally, the librarians faced a constant shortage of books, which came strictly from donations.

But the Kentucky pack horse librarians were determined. Every mile traveled brought new ideas and fresh interests to people in isolated areas. In 1937, one pack horse librarian, Gladys Lainhart, wrote, "It would be difficult to estimate how much this good work is doing to brighten the lives of the people in our Kentucky mountains."[3]

After Reading

Take Notes: Have students make a list of what they learned about the Kentucky Pack Horse Library Project. Invite students to compare lists with partners to see if they left out any key information.

Student Think Aloud

Use Copying Master number 7 to prompt students to share how they would summarize the story.

"This was mostly about . . ."

Cultural Perspective

People served by the Kentucky Pack Horse Library Project loved learning about other countries and cultures. Two of the most popular fiction books were *Robinson Crusoe* and *Gulliver's Travels*. *National Geographic* was one of the most requested magazines.

Think and Respond

1. What traits or skills do you think a woman needed to be a pack horse librarian? *Possible responses: She had to be brave to ride alone through dangerous areas and during bad weather. She had to be skilled at and enjoy riding horses because she had to ride about eighteen miles a day. She had to be friendly because some people did not trust the librarians.* **Critical**

2. Which parts of this selection were factual and which parts were fiction? *Possible response: The beginning of the selection when the authors wrote about the boy with the chipped tooth who speaks to the pack horse librarian is probably made up. The information about the pack horse library project is actually the truth.* **Genre**

3. What do you think the author wants readers to learn from this text? *Possible responses: I think the author wants us to learn how important many people think reading is. I think the author wants to tell us about how the librarians helped people who had lost their jobs and did not have money to buy books.* **Author's Purpose**

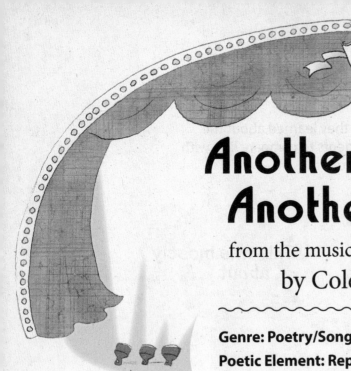

Another Op'nin', Another Show

from the musical *Kiss Me, Kate*

by Cole Porter

Genre: Poetry/Song
Poetic Element: Repetition and Rhyme
Comprehension Strategy: Summarize
Think-Aloud Copying Master number 7

Before Reading

Genre: Tell students you will read aloud lyrics to a song. Remind them that lyrics are meant to be sung to music. Tell students that this song is about people who act and sing in musical shows. Ask students to imagine what it would be like to move from city to city in order to put on shows for a living.

Expand Vocabulary: To help students better understand the lyrics, introduce the following terms:

> *op'nin'*: the shortened form of the word *opening;* refers to the first night of a new show
>
> *Philly, Baltimo'*: the shortened forms of Philadelphia and Baltimore
>
> *ulcers*: painful sores that are often caused by stress
>
> *overture*: the music that is played before the show begins

Set a Purpose for Reading: As students listen for details that relate to stage show entertainment, have them also note the repetition and rhyming patterns of the lyrics.

During Reading

To convey the excitement and anticipation of opening a new show, read expressively. Read through the song the first time without interruptions. Then reread, pausing to draw students' attention to the comprehension Think Aloud and genre note.

Another Op'nin', Another Show

from the musical *Kiss Me, Kate*
by Cole Porter

Another op'nin', another show
In Philly, Boston or Baltimo',
A chance for stage folks to say hello,
Another op'nin' of another show.
Another job that you hope, at last,
Will make your future forget your past,
Another pain where the ulcers grow,
Another op'nin' of another show.
Four weeks, you rehearse and rehearse,
Three weeks and it couldn't be worse,
One week, will it ever be right?
Then out o' the hat, it's that big first night!
The overture is about to start,
You cross your fingers and hold your heart,
It's curtain time and away we go![1]
Another op'nin',
Just another op'nin' of another show.
Another op'nin', another show
In Philly, Boston or Baltimo',
A chance for stage folks to say hello,
Another op'nin' of another show.
Another job that you hope, at last,
Will make your future forget your past,
Another pain where the ulcers grow,
Another op'nin' of another show.
Four weeks, you rehearse and rehearse,
Three weeks and it couldn't be worse,
One week, will it ever be right?
Then out o' the hat, it's that big first night!
The overture is about to start,
You cross your fingers and hold your heart,
It's curtain time and away we go!
Another op'nin',
Just another op'nin' of another show.

Think Aloud

[1] *I think this sums up the process of putting on a play or a show quite well. In our school, we spend weeks rehearsing for performances, too. It's quite stressful but exciting.*

After Reading

Set a Purpose for Rereading: Reread the song for the purpose of exploring how the speaker feels about the ongoing process of rehearsing and putting on shows.

Student Think Aloud

Use Copying Master number 7 to prompt students to share how the song sums up a long process in a short time.

"This was mostly about . . ."

Cultural Perspective

Lyricist Cole Porter learned how to play the piano and the violin when he was only six years old. He wrote hundreds of songs for Broadway musicals, movies, and television shows. *Kiss Me, Kate* was his most successful musical and ran for over one thousand performances.

Think and Respond

1. What details in the lyrics point out the hardships of working in show business? *Possible responses: It states you can get ulcers from the stress. There can be problems with the show only a few weeks before the opening.* **Analytical**

2. The songwriter uses the word *another* throughout the song. What effect does this create? *Possible responses: The people putting on the show go through the same experiences again and again. The work never ends because there is always another show to prepare for and perform.* **Poetic Element**

3. What do you think Cole Porter wants listeners to learn about the people who put on shows? *Possible responses: He wants to show that putting on a show is a lot of hard work. He wants to show the different emotions the performers have.* **Author's Purpose**

ON OUR OWN

from *Kon-Tiki: A True Adventure of Survival at Sea*
by Thor Heyerdahl

Genre: Narrative Nonfiction

Comprehension Strategy: Summarize

Think-Aloud Copying Master number 7

Before Reading

Genre: Tell students they will listen to a nonfiction narrative. Explain that this type of expository text is a story about events that actually happened. This means the author is writing about his or her own firsthand experiences, thoughts, and feelings.

Expand Vocabulary: Introduce the following words before reading to help students understand the selection:

current: a strong flow of water in the ocean

sheets: large flat surfaces

cork: a lightweight piece of material that floats and is used to close a bottle

cabin: a small room on a ship where people can take shelter

Set a Purpose for Reading: Have students listen for sensory details that help them understand what it was like to sail on the *Kon-Tiki*.

During Reading

Use the comprehension Think Alouds during the first reading of the story. Notes about the genre and cultural perspective may be used during subsequent readings.

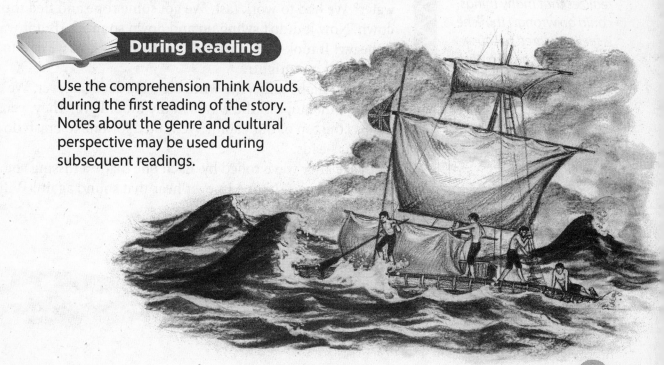

ON OUR OWN

from *Kon-Tiki: A True Adventure of Survival at Sea*
by Thor Heyerdahl

Kon-Tiki's sail filled with wind. The raft began to move forward. We were on our own at last!

Now that we were at sea, we began to worry. So many things could go wrong. People had warned us about all of them. The big logs of our raft might soak up water and sink. The ropes that held the logs together might break. A big wind might pick up our little raft and turn it over.

We had laughed at these warnings. Now they did not seem so funny. We could see how big the ocean was. We started to wonder. Was this trip a crazy idea after all?

It was too late to go back now. On that first afternoon a big wind blew up. A strong ocean current carried us along. We could not turn the raft around even if we wanted to. The *Kon-Tiki* had to go with the current. It could not ride against it. The waves around us were growing bigger and bigger. Soon the *Kon-Tiki* was bobbing up and down like a toy boat.[1]

Steering was our biggest problem. Our steering oar was nineteen feet long. It was very heavy and strong. But the waves were stronger. When a big wave hit the raft, the oar flew out of the water. It slammed against the men who were steering.

I was afraid. What if the oar broke? What if it fell into the water? We had to work fast. We got some rope and tied the oar down. Now it didn't swing up and down so much. But it was still so heavy! It took two of us together to steer. And we had to hang on with all our might.

When night came, the wind blew harder than ever. We could see the white tops of the waves in the moonlight. They were as high as the top of our cabin! We waited for one to crash down over our heads.

Wave after wave rolled by. Each one made a hissing sound as it rushed past. I hope I never hear that sound again! With

every wave, the back of the raft went up, up, up into the air.[2] Yet somehow we never tipped over.

We all took turns steering. The work was very hard. When a really big wave hit, the men at the oar had to let go. Then everybody just grabbed the side of the raft and held on tight.

Soon our legs were black and blue. Our arms ached. Our hands were bleeding.

We were all so tired from fighting the waves. But trying to sleep was very hard, too. The boat rocked so much that we could not rest. We had to tie a rope to our legs to keep from falling into the sea. Our sleeping bags were wet and cold. Our clothes were wet, too.

Poor Knut had the worst time of all. He was seasick. Soon he was too weak to work. He just sat in one corner of the raft. Our parrot sat right beside him. It was seasick, too!

The rough seas lasted for three days. Then the waves began to get smaller. "At last," I thought. "The worst is over."

But I was wrong! Early that morning it started to rain. The rain came down in sheets. It started all of a sudden. We had left one man holding the oar. The rain caught him by surprise. A big wave hit the raft. He let go for just one second. The *Kon-Tiki* spun around like a cork. When it stopped spinning, we were riding backward through the sea.

There was no way to turn the raft around. The rain almost tore our sail in half. We had to take it down to save it. We all saw that there was nothing more we could do. We were too tired to fight anymore. We had to get lucky now. We tied down everything on deck. One by one, we crawled into the little cabin.

Soon we all fell fast asleep.

The next thing we heard was the happy screaming of our parrot. It was the first sound the poor bird had made in days. We rubbed our eyes and looked outside. The sun was shining brightly. The sea was calm again. Now the ocean looked very friendly. Our first storm at sea was over. The *Kon-Tiki* had passed its first test.[3]

Think Aloud

[2]I noticed that the author used sensory details that help me imagine what it was like to ride on the raft. He said the waves made a hissing sound and he described how the raft was carried up very high by the waves.

Think Aloud

[3]I was glad to read that the crew survived. This last sentence sums up the story well. They had faced their first challenge at sea. The raft and its passengers made it through the frightening storm.

Retell the Story: Invite students to paraphrase the story of how the *Kon-Tiki* survived the first storm as if they had been on the raft. Remind them to use words like *I, me,* and *we* in their retelling.

Student Think Aloud

Use Copying Master number 7 to prompt students to share how they would sum up the story. What lessons do they think the crew learned during their ordeal?

"This was mostly about . . ."

Cultural Perspective

Thor Heyerdahl was a Norwegian explorer who wanted to prove that people from South America could have sailed a raft to the South Pacific. With a crew of five, he sailed for 101 days across 4,300 miles in the Pacific Ocean until they reached the Tuamotu Islands. Have students discuss other stories they have read about exploration. Ask them to share why this theme is universal across cultures and times.

Think and Respond

1. What do you think the people on the *Kon-Tiki* found to be the most difficult part of their journey? *Possible responses: not knowing if they would survive the storm; having aching arms and bloody hands from holding the oar; having a rope tied around your legs so you won't fall off the raft; not being able to sleep; being wet and cold all the time.* **Analytical**

2. What descriptive details does the author use to make the narrative come alive for readers? *Possible responses: He describes the sound of the waves and how they rocked the raft. He describes how people's legs were bruised, their arms ached, and their hands bled.* **Genre**

3. Why do you think Thor Heyerdahl chose to write about his experience at sea? *Possible response: I think he wants to share his incredible story with other people.* **Author's Purpose**

Small Artist Has a Big Appeal:
Show Features 12-Year-Old's Work
by Fabiola Santiago

Genre: Nonfiction/News Article

Comprehension Strategy: Analyze Text Structure

Think-Aloud Copying Master number 5

Before Reading

Genre: Tell students they will listen to a news article. Remind them that the purpose of a news article is to inform readers about a real event or person. Explain that most news articles answer these questions: *who, what, when, where,* and *why.*

Expand Vocabulary: Improve students' comprehension of the selection by introducing the following words before reading:

> *canvases:* large pieces of cloth on which artists paint
>
> *muse:* imaginary someone or something that inspires you
>
> *trance:* a sleep-like state a person experiences when concentrating very hard
>
> *collector:* someone who buys art as a hobby

Set a Purpose for Reading: Invite students to listen to find out who Alejandro Fernández is and what is special about him.

During Reading

Use the comprehension Think Alouds during the first reading of the article. Notes about the genre and cultural perspective may be used during subsequent readings.

Think Aloud

[1] I noticed that the author used contrast in the headline and the beginning of the article. I wonder why? Alejandro is only 12 years old and he is not tall enough to reach some of his canvases, but his paintings sell for the same prices as paintings created by adults. That must be the reason why.

Small Artist Has a Big Appeal:
Show Features 12-Year-Old's Work
by Fabiola Santiago

He's only 12, a cherubic-cheeked boy immersed in his first reading of *Oliver Twist* and not yet tall enough to reach some of the canvases before him.

But what Alejandro Fernández paints is commanding adult-size prices.[1]

"It's like this," Alejandro says, standing before two of his works going on display Friday at Coral Gables International Art Center, *Woman in a Hat* and *Woman in a Red Dress*, both priced at $6,000. "I have a muse, and when it descends, I go to my canvas and I start to search for what it is I want to do."

Woman in a Red Dress, for example, started out in blue.

"I wanted to paint a woman thinking, with her eyes closed and all her thoughts surrounding her," he says.

When he finished, he did what he always does—leave the painting alone for three or four days.

When he came back to it, it was all there for him, except for the color of the dress. He changed it to white, then red.

"I can't explain it," he says of his method, "but I search and I search, and something tells me when I have found it—and then I stop."

When he gets to a spot on the canvas he can't reach, Alejandro pulls up a chair, any chair, even a fancy dining room chair.

He stands on it and paints.

His parents let him; they wouldn't want to interrupt his trance.

"I don't think there's a spot in our house that doesn't have a brush stroke here and there," says father Victor Fernández.

Alejandro and his father say Alejandro paints mostly on Saturdays and Sundays when he doesn't have school (he just completed sixth grade)—and only until he feels like it—or say, until a game of basketball beckons.

"We don't push him at all," his father says. "We've never had to. Painting is just something he has chosen to do since he was small. We want to nurture his talent, but at the same time we are concerned about the pressures because he's so young."

Alejandro's resume is short—from paper and crayons to this first exhibit of acrylics on canvas—but his work has an exceptional Matisse-like flair that people like, says gallery owner Fred Castro.

"We've already sold three pieces," Castro says. "We put them up and they went right away. One <u>collector</u> who's a client bought two and another woman bought one."

The smaller artworks sold for $2,500 and $3,500; the larger *Woman in a Red Dress* went for $6,000, Castro says.

Castro is pledging to donate 20 percent of proceeds from Alejandro's exhibit to the non-profit Hands in Action, a child-abuse prevention center in Hialeah founded by another gallery artist, Carmen Portela, after her son was slain by a man who had been abused as a child.

Alejandro, who lives in Puerto Rico, started to paint when he was 5 and living in his native Santa Clara in central Cuba.[2]

He left Cuba just a year ago after he and his mother won the U.S. visa lottery and were able to join his dad, who left the island for Mexico and crossed the border into the United States hoping to later reunite his family.

The women in Alejandro's artwork are inspired by his one and only model—his mother, Marlén Finalé.[3]

"She looks beautiful and now she has a belly like this," he says of Marlén, who is expecting the family's second child.

Alejandro says he's seldom completely pleased with his finished pieces.

"I always think I can do something prettier," he says.

But his favorite is *The Violinist,* which he painted some years back and the family doesn't want to sell.

It adorns his parents' living room wall.

"It has a movement I really like," Alejandro says.

Summarize: Have students write a one-paragraph summary of the article. Remind them to include only the most important information in their summary as they answer the questions *who, what, when, where,* and *why.* Later, have students discuss their responses to the article and their opinions about Alejandro.

Student Think Aloud

Use Copying Master number 5 to prompt students to discuss the structure of the story and how it helped their understanding.

"I noticed the author used . . ."

Cultural Perspective

Through the Diversity Visa Lottery Program, the United States awards 50,000 immigrant visas each year to people from other countries. The visas allow them to live and work permanently in America. None of these visas are available for people who come from countries that have sent more than 50,000 immigrants to the United States within the past five years. Have students identify other cultural elements in the article.

Think and Respond

1. In what ways is Alejandro like a typical 12-year-old boy? In what ways is he like an adult? *Possible responses: He goes to school and plays basketball. He paints pictures that are displayed in art galleries and that people want to buy.* **Analytical**

2. What do the quotations from Alejandro, his father, and the gallery owner add to the news article? *Possible responses: They let readers hear the artist talk about his work in his own words. They add interest to the article because readers learn more about Alejandro from his father and the gallery owner.* **Genre**

3. Why do you think Fabiola Santiago chose to write about Alejandro? *Possible responses: Perhaps she thought people would be interested to learn about him and his art. Alejandro is an interesting topic for an article because he is a young boy who paints and sells his art for a lot of money.* **Author's Purpose**

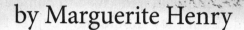

Misty of Chincoteague

by Marguerite Henry

Genre: Fiction/Novel

Comprehension Strategy: Analyze Text Structure

Think-Aloud Copying Master number 5

Before Reading

Genre: Tell students that you will read aloud an excerpt or section of a classic novel. Explain that a classic novel features memorable characters in a story that has stood the test of time. This means that readers can relate to and enjoy the story because it touches them or deals with ideas or themes that they care about today. Tell students that although this story has fictional characters, it is based on an annual event. The pony round-up is still held each year on the last Wednesday of July.

Expand Vocabulary: Introduce the following words students may find challenging:

> *game warden:* a person who is in charge of protecting the animals in a specific area
>
> *withers:* the ridge between a horse's shoulder bones
>
> *got poor:* became sickly due to lack of food
>
> *rustle her feed:* manage to find food to eat
>
> *filly:* a young female horse
>
> *corral:* a pen or enclosure where horses are kept

Set a Purpose for Reading: Invite students to listen for ways in which the author shows emotion and creates tone, mood, and suspense in the story.

During Reading

Use the comprehension Think Alouds during the first reading of the story. Notes about the genre and cultural perspective may be used during subsequent readings.

Misty of Chincoteague

by Marguerite Henry

Genre Study

Fiction/Classic Novel: The author has piqued the readers' interest, drawn them into the plot of the story, and made them want to find out what happens next. The children's desire to go off in search of adventure is a recurring theme with which many people can identify.

Think Aloud

[1]*I notice the author uses the setting to create a mood or feeling right away in this excerpt. The two characters are on an island and are exploring a ship's graveyard. It is quiet and the children are all alone. There aren't even any animals around. That sounds like a spooky place.*

The girl looked around and about her. Everything was still and quiet on little Assateague Island. Their grandfather had brought the game warden to the island in his boat, and she and Paul had asked to come along. But now she wondered if they should have come. The men were seeing how the wild birds had weathered the winter. They were far to the north. No other creatures were in sight. Suddenly she felt a little chill of fear.

"Paul," she asked in a hushed voice, "do you feel like we're trespassing?"

Paul nodded. "If you look close," he whispered, "you can see that the wild critters have 'No Trespassing' signs tacked up on every pine tree."

"I wasn't thinking about the wild things," Maureen replied. She shielded her eyes against the sun and looked off in the direction of Tom's Cove. "Wish Grandpa'd come to take us back home to Chincoteague. It seems spooky-like to be exploring a ship's graveyard."[1]

"I like exploring. I don't care if . . ."

Suddenly, from the pine thicket behind them came the sharp crackling of underbrush. Paul wheeled around, his eyes darting to an open glade.

"Watch the open place, Maureen! It's the Pied Piper and his band!"

With manes and tails flying, a band of wild ponies swept into the natural grazing ground. A pinto stallion was in command. He bunched his mares, then tossed his head high, searching the wind.

Paul and Maureen fell to the sand. They did not want the wind to carry their scent. They watched as the stallion herded his family like a nervous parent on a picnic. When he made certain that no one was missing, he began browsing. It was like a signal. His mares lowered their heads and settled down to the business of grazing.

Paul's eyes were fixed on the wild horses. They were cropping grass peacefully. But he knew that one strange sound would send them rocketing off into the woods. He and Maureen spoke softly and scarcely moved.

"Do y'see the Phantom?" asked Maureen.

The very mention of the name "Phantom" set Paul's heart thumping against the walls of his chest.[2] That mysterious wild mare about whom so many stories were told!

"No," he answered. "They're bunched too close."

"Do you reckon the Phantom's real? Or do you reckon it was some sea monster upset that boat last roundup?"

Paul gave no answer. Was the Phantom real? Sometimes he wondered. She had never been captured, and the roundup men did sometimes tell tall tales. Some had said she was a dark creature, dark and mysterious, like the pine trees. And some said she was the color of copper, with splashes of silver in her mane and tail. And some spoke of a strange white marking that began at her <u>withers</u> and spread out like a white map of the United States.[3]

"Maybe," whispered Maureen, "maybe she <u>got poor</u> and died off during the winter."

"Her?" scoffed Paul, his eyes never leaving the herd. "Not her! Any pony that can outsmart Grandpa and all the roundup men for two years running can <u>rustle her feed,</u> all right. Remember how Uncle Jed said his horse broke a leg trying to follow the Phantom at the roundup last Pony Penning Day?"

"Wish girls could go along on the roundup; maybe she wouldn't bolt away from another girl."

Paul snorted. "She'd leap into the waves and swim out to sea just like she did last year and the year before that." Then suddenly his face lighted as if an idea had just struck him. "But this year it's going to be different."

"Why is it?"

"Because," Paul replied, gripping the rib bone in his hand, "because I'm old enough to go with the roundup men this year. That's why. And if there is such a <u>filly,</u> I'm going to get her, and on Pony Penning Day she'll be in the <u>corral</u> with the others."

Think Aloud

[2] I can figure out that Phantom is the name of a wild horse the children have heard about in stories. The author says that Paul's heart is beating very hard. I wonder if this means that he is afraid of Phantom or that he is excited about the possibility of seeing the wild horse.

Think Aloud

[3] I wonder if the Phantom is a real horse. Paul says the men tell tall tales, and I know that these types of stories are not usually about real people or events. The author creates a sense of mystery about the horse by including details from these stories. This makes me want to read on to find out the truth about the Phantom, just like Paul and Maureen.

After Reading

Retell the Story: Have students role-play the story. Invite them to add their own dialogue to include Maureen's reaction to Paul's claim that he will be the one to capture the Phantom.

Student Think Aloud

Use Copying Master number 5 to prompt students to discuss how the author presents important information about the main characters, the setting, the plot, or the tale of the Phantom.

"I noticed the author used . . ."

Cultural Perspective

Assateague and Chincoteague Islands are located just off the coast of Virginia. One popular explanation for how the horses got to Assateague Island is that a Spanish ship on its way to South America crashed on the shore in the 1500s. The horses escaped the ship, and later generations continued to make the island their home.

Think and Respond

1. Based on what you have read, do you think Paul will be able to capture the Phantom on Pony Penning Day? Why or why not? *Possible responses: No; if the men can't capture the horse, how will a boy be able to do it? Yes; he seems very confident and determined.* **Inferential**

2. Identify the main characters, setting, and plot of this selection. *Possible responses: The main characters are a boy and a girl named Paul and Maureen. The setting is Assateague Island. The story is about two kids who are exploring an island and watching a band of wild ponies.* **Genre**

3. Why do you think the author doesn't tell readers whether the Phantom is a real horse or just a character in a tall tale? *Possible response: The author creates a sense of mystery by making readers wonder if the horse really exists. This makes readers want to continue the story and find out the truth.* **Author's Purpose**

The Golden Wish

a *Greek myth*

retold by Geraldine McCaughrean

Genre: Myth

Comprehension Strategy: Analyze Story Structure

Think-Aloud Copying Master number 5

Before Reading

Genre: Tell students you will read aloud a Greek myth about King Midas. Remind students that the characters in Greek myths include humans, gods and goddesses, and imaginary creatures. Explain that the purpose of some myths is to teach a lesson about human behavior. Myths were also created by people to explain things in the world around them.

Expand Vocabulary: Introduce the following words to help students better understand the selection:

> *vaults:* rooms made to store money and other valuables
>
> *unconquerable:* cannot be defeated
>
> *blighted:* harmed, destroyed
>
> *alchemy:* the ability to turn something common into something valuable

Set a Purpose for Reading: Invite students to listen for enjoyment and to find out how and why King Midas acted foolishly.

During Reading

Use the comprehension Think Alouds during the first reading of the story. Notes about the genre and cultural perspective may be used during subsequent readings.

The Golden Wish

a Greek myth
retold by Geraldine McCaughrean

There was once a fool. Of course there have been far more fools than one, and fools more often than once. But this particular fool was a king, so his foolishness mattered. He lived in Greece, at the foot of Mount Olympus, and his name was Midas. All he thought about was gold. All day, while the golden sun shone, he shut himself away in dark vaults counting his gold. All night long, while the golden firelight glimmered, he shivered over his accounting books reading the words to himself:[1]

> Twelve bars of gold in my vaults
> Twenty plates of gold on my table
> Ten rings of gold on my wife
> Four hundred gold coins in my tax coffers . . .

The centaurs, unlike Midas, valued only fun. One day (and on many others, too) darkness surprised a centaur after a day of adventures, and he gratefully stumbled upon Midas's garden.

"I am lost," he told the king.

Midas set the centaur on the right road for Olympus.

"Such a friend! Such kindness!" exclaimed the centaur, joyfully kicking up his heels. "How can I thank you? A wish? I shall grant you one wish."

Now Midas knew that these centaurs, these horse-men, grazed on the slopes of Olympus and drew magic from the holy mountain. His heart leapt to his mouth. "A wish? You mean anything? I wish that everything I touch turns to gold!" He said it quickly, before the centaur could withdraw the offer.

"Ah. I should have warned you. People have asked that of the gods before, and . . ."

"Your magic isn't powerful enough! I knew it."

"Oh, I can grant it," said the centaur, flicking flies with his long tail. "But you'll be sorry."

"No, I won't!"

The centaur pronounced no spell. He did not spit or clap or chant. So when he trotted away toward Olympus, Midas felt sure no magic had passed between them. "Boaster! Braggart!"

he yelled after the galloping horse-man, and pounded the garden wall with his fist.

The wall felt smooth under his hand. It gleamed and glittered in the sunlight.

Gold.

Midas ran to his treasury and touched all the brass coins. They instantly shone gold—and not just the coins, but the jars they were in and the door of the treasure-house.

Gold.

Midas ran through the palace stroking and slapping every stool, bench, table and urn. They all turned to gold. His china and statues, his weapons and chariot all shone, more exquisite and precious than anything he had ever dreamed of owning. "When we charge into battle," he told his horse, patting its fat rump, "we shall dazzle our enemies, you and I!"

The horse did not respond. It stood quite silent and quite still between the traces of the chariot: a perfect gold statue of a horse. Midas was a little startled, but after a moment he shrugged his shoulders. It made a fine statue for his new golden palace. And fresh horses can be bought by the dozen if a man has the gold to buy them.

"A feast! A festival! Where's my Chancellor? Where's my cook? Invite everyone! Spare no expense! Let the world know that Midas has gold! Midas has gold enough to buy up every sword, every horse, every acre of land in the world! I shall be unconquerable! I shall be worshiped! I shall be the envy of every man from the poorest beggar to the richest millionaire![2] I shall be the richest millionaire! A millionaire a million times over! Cook, where are you?"

His cook rushed in, carrying the King's lunch. He could not help but stare around him at all the changes to the room—the gold ornaments, the golden furniture. Midas snatched the bread impatiently off the tray and bit it. "Huh? What are you feeding me these days? Rocks?" When he threw down the bread in disgust, it skidded across the golden floor. A golden loaf.

Food too, then? Midas took a drink to steady his nerves.

At least, he tried to take a drink. But the wine, as it touched his lip, turned to gold, to solid, metallic, unyielding gold. Midas stared. The cook stared. "Don't just stand there! Fetch me something I can eat!" And he gave the man a push.

Think Aloud

[2]*I think this dialogue is important because it tells me a lot about the king's character. All he cares about is getting as much wealth as he can so he can make other people jealous. It does not seem as if he values anything else in his life.*

Ah well, there are more cooks in the world, for a man with limitless gold.

Midas sat down on the ground beside the golden statue of his cook. His clothes, one by one, in touching his skin, had been turning to gold around him, and he found that he was suddenly very, very weary from wearing them.

He had not meant it to be like this when he asked the centaur to . . . He had not meant food and clothes and people and horses . . .

Midas began to wonder. How long does it take for a man to starve to death?

Just then, his queen came in and, ahead of her, their little daughter. Midas tried to warn her. He tried to stop the girl running to him with outstretched arms. But the child was too young to understand. Her little fingers closed around Midas's hand—and stiffened, and grew cold, and could not be pried open again. Her face and features, too, hardened and set, and the eyes were plain gold orbs in their golden sockets, the golden mouth frozen, forever half-open to speak.

"Oh Zeus! Oh you gods! No! Not my daughter! Not my little girl!" He ran past the Queen, past the guards, his arms burdened with the monstrous weight of a small clinging golden child. He ran out of his golden palace and its golden gardens: the flower heads jangled as he brushed by them. He ran across golden grass to a forest and blighted it with a golden canker. He ran through orchards till the sight of the fruit maddened him with hunger. He started up the rocky slopes of Olympus, staggering under the weight of his lifeless daughter.

How long does it take for a man to die of loneliness? Or a broken heart?

"Take back this curse! What did I ever do to you that you punish me like this?" When he kicked off his heavy golden shoes, the golden grass spiked his soles like needles.[3]

"Curse? I thought I granted you a wish," said a familiar voice. The centaur trotted out of a nearby cave.

"I was a fool! I see that now! I was a fool! But does a man deserve to lose his daughter—to die—just because he's a fool?"

The centaur picked a few stalks of grass and nibbled them thoughtfully. "I did try to warn you. Perhaps I've done you a favor, after all, if it has taught you something about yourself . . ."

"Wonderful! I shall die wise, then!" said Midas.

Think Aloud

[3]I am able to picture in my mind the grass stabbing the king's feet. The author paints this picture by comparing the grass to golden needles. The image helps me to visualize the action.

The centaur blew through his lips. "If you take my advice, you'll go to the river and jump in," he said.

"*Kill* myself, you mean?" gasped Midas.

"No, you fool. *Wash* yourself."

At the banks of the river, Midas did not hesitate. If the water did not turn to gold and crush him, then the weight of the metal child clasping his hand might pull him under and drown him. But he did not care. He flung himself into the river, and its water closed over his head. As he surfaced, his daughter surfaced beside him, spluttering and terrified, not knowing why or how she came to be swimming. "Father? How did we get here?"

Together they carried buckets of water back to the palace, and flung it over cook and horse, over stool and table and coins. The color of gold was loathsome to Midas, and he was not content until he had undone all the <u>alchemy</u> of his magic golden touch.

Never again did he dream of gold—except in nightmares. Never again did he yearn to own gilded ornaments and mounds of yellow riches. No, no! For Midas had learned his lesson, hadn't he?

Now he thought about jewels, instead.

Retell the Story: Have students act out the story. Ask them to include a part for the king's wife and show her reaction to his new golden touch.

Student Think Aloud

Use Copying Master number 5 to prompt students to share their thoughts about the structure and elements of the myth.

"I noticed the author used . . ."

Cultural Perspective

There really was a King Midas who was king of Phrygia (what is today part of Turkey) in the eighth century. There was also a river near his kingdom. Some people believe this myth was created to explain why people found flakes of gold in this river.

Think and Respond

1. Do you think King Midas really learned his lesson? Do you think he will ever ask for another wish? Why or why not? *Possible responses: No, because he would not want to risk the life of his family ever again. Yes; I think he is already thinking of asking for jewels next time.* **Analytical**

2. What character traits of King Midas teach us how we should not be? *Possible responses: Greedy—he spends all his time counting his money and thinking about getting more. Arrogant—he refuses to listen to the centaur's warning about his wish. Hasty—he doesn't consider the consequences of his wish.* **Genre**

3. Why do people still listen to myths like this one today? What was the author's purpose? *Possible responses: They are entertaining and have magical creatures. Their lessons are still important to people today. This myth teaches us that greed can be dangerous. It teaches us that one does not need to be rich to be happy.* **Author's Purpose**

Darkness Is My Friend

from Mouse Tail Moon
by Joanne Ryder

Genre: Poetry
Poetic Element: Metaphor
Comprehension Strategy: Analyze Text Structure
Think-Aloud Copying Master number 5

 Before Reading

Genre: Explain to students that a narrative poem tells a story. Tell students that the narrative poem that you are about to read aloud contains figurative language. Remind students that a metaphor is a comparison between two things that at first may not seem to have anything in common. Explain that poets use figurative language to develop meaning. Once students have read "Long Trip" by Langston Hughes, explain that it also uses metaphor; it compares the sea to a desert and a wilderness. Point out that the following poem compares darkness to a friend.

Expand Vocabulary: Introduce the following words before reading:

rustle: make a light noise like dry leaves blowing in the wind

outsiders: people who are not included in a certain group

lend: loan or provide

Set a Purpose for Reading: Have students listen and watch the reader to identify tone, mood, and emotion in verbal and nonverbal communication.

 **During Reading**

Read through the poem without interruptions. Then reread, pausing to draw students' attention to the comprehension Think Aloud and genre note.

Genre Study

Narrative Poetry: Poets sometimes have characters use imperfect grammar when they speak because it sounds more realistic. The speaker of this narrative poem says *who* instead of *whom*.

Think Aloud

[1] *I wonder who or what the speaker is. The poet uses both short and long sentences to give clues to the speaker's identity. Some words and phrases repeat. I know the speaker is small and is active at night. Is the speaker a person or an animal? I will continue listening for more clues.*

Darkness Is My Friend

from *Mouse Tail Moon*

by Joanne Ryder

Darkness is my friend.
No one sees me.
Darkness is my friend.
I am small.
In the night I know
darkness hides me,
and I feel much braver and tall.[1]
All around, I hear others like me.
We are those
who darkness sets free.
We are those
who rustle and whisper,
living lives outsiders won't see.
We are born and die
in the darkness,
sharing comfort shadows can lend—
melting in the
brightness of daylight
when the nighttime
comes to its end.
In the dark
I too am a shadow.
Darkness is my friend.

Set a Purpose for Rereading: Once you have read the poem aloud for students' enjoyment, reread it for the purpose of exploring the poet's use of figurative language.

Student Think Aloud

Use Copying Master number 5 to prompt students to discuss the poem's structure and how the poet uses it to make her point.

"I noticed the author used . . ."

Think and Respond

1. Who or what is the speaker? What clues in the poem helped you figure this out? *Although the speaker is in fact a mouse, accept any reasonable responses, including a nighttime creature or any creature (animal or human) who fears exposure to daylight or fears being seen or discovered by "outsiders." Possible response: The poet says the speaker is small, comes out at night with others like it, stays hidden from outsiders, searches for food, makes soft noises, and fears the light of daytime.* **Analytical**

2. What do you normally think of when describing a friend? In the poem, why does the speaker compare darkness to a friend? *Possible responses: A friend is a person you like and whose presence makes you feel safe. A friend is someone who looks out for you. The narrator calls darkness a friend because it helps him or her hide. This helps the speaker feel safe and more daring.* **Poetic Element**

3. How does the poet make us think about nighttime and darkness in a new way? *Possible responses: Many people normally think of nighttime as a scary time because you cannot see in the dark. In this poem, the narrator enjoys nighttime because it is when he or she feels most confident. Darkness gives the speaker freedom because he or she can hide.* **Author's Purpose**

MARY ANNING AND THE SEA DRAGON

by Jeannine Atkins

Genre: Biography

Comprehension Strategy: Generate Questions

Think-Aloud Copying Master number 1

Before Reading

Genre: Tell students they will listen to a biographical sketch with some fictional elements added for interest. Explain that this type of text tells a story about real people and real events. The author has created dialogue and the smaller details of the story. She also gives a realistic account of Mary Anning, her family, and her incredible discovery.

Expand Vocabulary: Introduce the following words before reading:

   curiosities: unusual items found in nature

   pounds: a type of money used in England

   pry: remove with difficulty

   trade: a type of work that requires special skill

Set a Purpose for Reading: Invite students to listen for information about the life of Mary Anning.

During Reading

Use the comprehension Think Alouds during the first reading of the story. Notes about the genre and cultural perspective may be used during subsequent readings.

MARY ANNING AND THE SEA DRAGON

by Jeannine Atkins

Mary Anning knew from the sound of the sea that the tide was going out. She was eager to search the shore for stone sea lilies and shells, but she had to watch her younger brothers while Mother worked.

Mary put more driftwood on the fire. Then she spoke slowly to her brothers as she made shadows of sea dragons on the wall. Getting to the end of a story quicker wouldn't bring her mother home any sooner.

But the minute her mother entered the cottage, Mary called their dog, Blackie, and grabbed her bonnet, basket, and tools. The sign reading GIFTS AND <u>CURIOSITIES</u> thudded against the door as Mother followed her outside, shouting, "Wait!"

Mother took Mary's straw bonnet and replaced it with a top hat.

"It's a gentleman's hat! It's not proper for a girl," Mary complained, repeating what her mother had said when Father was alive.

"It will keep your head safe from falling rocks, Mary," Mother said. That was what Father used to say. Sturdy top hats protected riders when they were flung from their horses. Mother tucked a flower into Mary's hatband and whispered, "Someday you'll wear the finest hat in town."

Mary kissed her mother goodbye and raced down to the seashore. When she reached the blue-gray cliffs, she raised her arms to feel the breeze beneath them, imagining that she was flying. Then she set to work, looking along the beach for stone curiosities and shells to sell to the people from the city who came here for the sea air.

After Mary's father had died last year when she was ten, Mary quit school to help earn money. Mother sold most of Father's carpentry tools to buy food. The saw and measures were gone, but Mary would never forget the way Father had walked with her through the woods so that she'd know where his chairs and tables had come from. "Everything starts from something living," he'd said. "If you look hard, you can see the tree that's in a table."[1]

So Mary looked hard, as usual. She climbed over stones that the rain and wind had broken from the cliffs. She looked until she spotted some markings on a wide, flat stone. She chipped

with her chisel and hammer. The lines seemed to form a tooth. She'd found teeth before. The tourists rarely bought them. Mary marked the spot and moved on to look for something prettier.

Before long, Mary found a snakestone. Its outline was as faint as a shadow. She chiseled away the softer stone around it, brushed off the dust, cut the snakestone from the rock, and dropped it into her basket. Then she straightened her back, looking at the cliffs where her father had fallen. The fall had worsened the cough Father died from, but he'd never hated the cliffs or the storms that loosened the rocks. There was something in the broken stones that he'd been searching for.

Mary hurried back to the spot she had marked. What if there wasn't just one tooth but a row of them? Mary chipped gently. Another shape like the first appeared. Mary was certain now that these were teeth, but of what creature? A wave touched her skirt, warning her that it was time to leave the beach. Once the tide swept in, there was nowhere to stand between the cliffs and the cold, fierce sea.

During the following weeks, Mary hunted for curiosities to sell. She also spent part of each day chiseling stone from a row of teeth that was growing longer and longer. Above the sound of the waves she heard her tapping and brushing, then a hush while she examined what she'd uncovered. Finally, a face about four feet long emerged from beneath her hands and knees.[2]

Mary brought her family to see it.

"Ugh, a crocodile!" her cousin Sarah said.

"What would a crocodile be doing in England?" asked Mary's older brother, Joseph. "It's a sea dragon!"

"Even if there's more to this sea dragon and she can get it out, who on earth would want it in their parlor?" Aunt Ruth frowned. "People already gossip about the way Mary runs around with a hammer and chisel and that silly hat. Her skirts are soaked."

"Clothing dries," Mary's mother said.

"When is she going to stop?" Aunt Ruth demanded.

"I expect she'll stop when she's finished." Mother squeezed Mary's hand. She seemed to know that Mary couldn't leave this etched stone any more than a nurse could turn from a patient, or an artist abandon a half-finished painting.

All winter, Mary worked with chapped, red hands. Her cloak flapped in the wind. *Don't ever stop looking, Mary.* Examining the shapes of bones, Mary heard her father's voice as clearly as if he were speaking to her now.

Think Aloud

[2] *I wonder what kind of creature the face belongs to. By not answering my question yet, the author builds suspense to get me to read further.*

Spring arrived, and a backbone emerged. Then a wing, or was it a fin or a paddle? The more Mary worked, the more she wondered: How long ago was long ago? What was here before us?

One June night, Mary's mother answered a knock at the cottage door.

"I'd like to speak to Miss Anning." A gentleman took off his tall hat and glanced into the shop. "I'm Lord Henley. My family's here on holiday, and some children took me to see what they call a sea dragon. Is it true that the lady who found it lives here?"

"You must want my daughter." Mother proudly nodded at Mary.

The gentleman looked surprised to find himself facing a girl who'd just turned twelve. Then he smiled and said, "Fossils are an interest of mine, too."

"Fossils?" Mary said.

"Fossils are traces of old life left in stone. What you call curiosities," Lord Henley explained. "Do you know what it is you've found, miss?"

"No, sir. Do you?"

"All I know is that it must be thousands of years old. Maybe millions. We can learn a lot about the Earth from something like this," Lord Henley said. "I'll give you ten <u>pounds</u> for it now and another ten when you get it out. That thing is already bigger than any of us, but I expect you'll find a way to <u>pry</u> it out. You seem to know your <u>trade</u>."

Encouraged by the prospect of more money than the Anning family had ever had, Joseph took time off from his job at a quarry to help Mary. But his hands were used to hammering hard and fast. His fingers were too rough to feel the slight impressions in the stone.

Some friends also wanted to help and borrowed tools from the blacksmith and stonemasons. But they found the work dull.

Soon Mary worked alone again. She remained alert to changes in the stone's hardness, listening when her hammer hit the chisel. A faint sound told her to alter the chisel's angle or she risked cracking the part of the rock that she was trying to save.

In one day she usually exposed an area half the size of her hand. But Mary forgot her own time as millions of the earth's years fell away.

Genre Study

Biography: A biographical sketch typically includes information about a certain person, his or her family, place of residence, education, occupation, life and activities. Sometimes an author adds some elements of fiction to make the story more interesting.

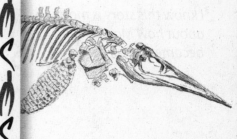

Late in the summer, almost a year after she'd begun, Mary worked with Joseph and some of his friends to remove the fossil from the surrounding stone. They cut the creature into slabs, which they carried on blankets to a horse and wagon.

Almost everyone in town came to watch. Tourists peered over one another's shoulders as much to see Mary as to see the fossil.

Lord Henley shook Mary's hand. He said, "Nothing like this has ever been found in England."

"At least you're done with that, Mary," Aunt Ruth said. "Now will you settle down to a normal life?"

Mary touched the fossil for courage, the way she had once reached for her mother's hand. There were creatures no one had ever thought existed. There were worlds no one had ever dreamed of. "I have work to do," Mary said.

Later, Mary watched the horse and wagon pull the fossil past the shops on Broad Street. Someday maybe she would go to London to see it displayed in a museum. She'd buy a splendid bonnet for her mother, but she'd keep her tall black hat. And she'd return to this shore to look for fossils, to hear the wind and her father's voice: *Don't ever stop looking, Mary.*[3]

Think Aloud

[3] *I know this story is mostly about how Mary Anning became a fossil collector.*

Retell the Story: Make a list of the key details you learned about Mary and her incredible discovery. Use your notes to write a newspaper article summarizing the events in the story.

Student Think Aloud

"I wonder . . ."

Use Copying Master number 1 to prompt students to share questions they had about the text and its subject matter.

Cultural Perspective

Mary Anning lived in a small village called Lyme Regis on the coast of England. The snakestones Mary finds in the story are actually fossils of ammonites—small, tubelike, shelled creatures that lived in the ocean. Discuss with students the historical and social aspects of this nonficton from another time.

Think and Respond

1. How does Mary's mother feel about her fossil collecting? How do you know this? *Possible responses: Her mother approves of Mary's fossil hunting. I know this because she squeezes Mary's hand to support her and offer courage. She also shows her pride in Mary when Lord Henley comes to their house.* **Inferential**

2. Which parts of the story are based on fact? Which parts are fictional? *Possible responses: Mary Anning was a real person who lived in Lyme Regis. She did find fossils, and her family members helped. But the author made up the dialogue and Mary's thoughts and feelings.* **Genre**

3. Why do you think the author ends the story with the words of Mary's father? *Possible responses: It shows that Mary will continue to pursue her explorations and do something she enjoys even though some people do not approve of it. It shows that Mary remembers the wisdom her father taught her.* **Author's Purpose**

The Flying Fool

by Thomas Fleming

Genre: Nonfiction/Expository

Comprehension Strategy: Generate Questions

Think-Aloud Copying Master number 1

Before Reading

Genre: Tell students you will read aloud a nonfiction selection. Remind them that the purpose of expository writing is to inform. The author of this selection uses specific details, including facts and figures, to give readers a firsthand account of Charles Lindbergh's historic flight from New York to Paris.

Expand Vocabulary: To help students understand this historic event, introduce the following words and phrases:

>*aviator:* a pilot, someone who flies airplanes

>*barrel rolls and loops:* names of movements an airplane can make in the air

>*flares:* emergency devices that can be lit to signal someone or attract attention

>*mirage:* an image of something that is not really there

Set a Purpose for Reading: Have students listen to find out the amazing details of Lindbergh's flight across the Atlantic from New York to Paris, France.

During Reading

Use the comprehension Think Alouds during the first reading of the story. Notes about the genre and cultural perspective may be used during subsequent readings.

The Flying Fool

by Thomas Fleming

In 1927, airplane travel was still something new. No one had ever even flown an airplane from the United States to mainland Europe.

One New York hotel owner wanted to challenge some brave pilot to do so. He offered a $25,000 prize to the first <u>aviator</u> who flew nonstop across the Atlantic between New York and Paris.

Among the competitors was Admiral Richard Byrd, who had recently flown over the North Pole with a three-man crew in a huge trimotor plane that cost $100,000. Two World War I French aces, Charles Nungesser and François Coli, were planning to fly from Paris. Also in the game was Clarence Chamberlin and his co-pilot, who had recently broken the world's record for endurance flying by staying aloft for 51 hours. Another two-man team was readying a plane with the backing of the American Legion.

Then there was Charles A. Lindbergh, a 25-year-old air-mail pilot from Minnesota. He was planning to fly the 3,636 miles alone in a single-engine plane called the *Spirit of St. Louis*. Newspapers nicknamed him "The Flying Fool." How could he compete?

A Parade of Failures

Lindbergh already had a reputation as a daring pilot. He had performed hair-raising <u>barrel rolls and loops</u> at county fairs. He had flown the mail between Chicago and St. Louis in all kinds of weather. But this was to be his most dangerous stunt yet.

To succeed, Lindbergh decided the plane had to be as light as possible. He supervised every step of its construction in San Diego, Calif. He eliminated the windshield and put two fuel tanks in the nose. He reduced his equipment to a minimum: a 10-pound rubber raft, a knife, some <u>flares</u>, a flashlight, a fishing line and hook, some chocolate rations. The main thing the plane would carry besides the 170-pound pilot was 451 gallons of gas.

In April 1927, Admiral Byrd's trimotor crashed on a test flight. The American Legion plane also crashed on takeoff, killing both pilots. The landing gear on Clarence Chamberlin's plane collapsed, and the craft nosed into the ground on a test run. All had the same problem. With the fuel needed for a transatlantic flight, they were too heavy.

As Lindbergh prepared to fly from San Diego to New York in the *Spirit of St. Louis*, Nungesser and Coli took off from Paris. Before he landed in New York, Lindbergh discovered the two Frenchmen had been lost somewhere in the Atlantic.[1]

Up, Up, and Away

Storms over the Atlantic delayed Lindbergh for almost two weeks. This gave Byrd and Chamberlin time to repair their planes. Would they take off when the weather cleared? No one was sure what was going to happen next.

On Thursday, May 19, the weather bureau reported it was clearing over the ocean but rain and wind would continue in New York. Lindbergh went to bed in a Long Island hotel, not far from where his plane was waiting. He could not sleep. He got up at 2:30 A.M. and drove through the rain to the airfield, where a big crowd was waiting for him.

Excitement grew as mechanics hauled the plane to nearby Roosevelt Field, which had a longer runway. "It was more like a funeral procession than the beginning of a flight to Paris," Lindbergh later recalled.

Lindbergh sat in the plane trying to decide whether to take off, while the rain fell around him. Not until daybreak, after reading more weather reports, did Lindbergh decide to go. Now came the real suspense. Could the *Spirit of St. Louis* get off the ground, loaded with 451 gallons of gasoline?[2]

Lindbergh had never tested the plane with that much fuel in its tanks. Halfway down the runway, Lindbergh still wasn't sure the plane would make it into the air. Seconds now to decide, he warned himself. The wrong decision meant a crash, probably in flames.

He pulled the stick back firmly. The wheels left the ground. Then they touched down again. He was almost at flying speed. It was too late to stop now. There was a web of telephone wires on poles at the end of the runway. He had to clear them.

Water splashed against the plane as it tore through a big puddle on the runway. The plane lifted off again—and came back down with the left wing low. Lindbergh leveled it as the plane hit another puddle. Airborne again, he let the wheels touch once more. "A little bow to earth, a gesture of humility," he called it.

The next time, the *Spirit of St. Louis* stayed in the air and cleared the telephone lines by 20 feet. The Flying Fool was on his way to Paris.

Can He Stay Awake?

When Lindbergh took off, he had not slept for 24 hours. Many people doubted he could stay awake for his lonely flight, which would take an estimated 36 hours. By this time the whole world was watching. Ships reported seeing him off Cape Cod heading toward Nova Scotia. He flew low, sometimes only 10 feet above the water, to save gas and keep his mind alert.

Nova Scotia was the first test of his navigation. Lindbergh was relieved to find he was only six miles off course. But after eight hours, his eyes began to feel "dry and hard as stones." He forced them open, then squeezed them shut again and again.

Night fell as he flew over Newfoundland. Below him ghostly white icebergs appeared by the dozens. Realizing he had a tailwind, which would increase his air speed, Lindbergh decided he had enough gasoline to climb to 10,000 feet. Suddenly huge clouds loomed ahead. It became very cold in the cockpit. Lindbergh stuck his hand out the side window and felt sleet sting his skin. He grabbed a flashlight and saw ice forming on one of the wing struts. If it formed on the wings he was doomed.

Wind lashed the plane. The two compasses on which he depended for navigation stopped working. At one point a fierce gust turned the plane completely around. Abruptly the clouds separated, and up ahead Lindbergh saw moonlight. As he crossed the halfway mark of his flight, the ice vanished from his struts. His compasses began working again.

After 17 hours in the air, Lindbergh's body ached. His face burned. He was desperate for sleep. He dived low enough to let spray from whitecaps douse his face. Another time, he let light rain blow into the cockpit to keep him awake. At one point, he looked down and saw a whole continent off his left wing— a <u>mirage</u>.

Suddenly he saw fishing boats below him. On one he saw a man staring up at him. Lindbergh spiraled down and shouted: "Which way is Ireland?" Getting no answer, he flew on. He began to see gulls. More land loomed ahead. It was Ireland! He was only three miles off course!

Genre Study

Nonfiction/ Expository: The author used old interviews and newspaper articles in which Lindbergh describes the famous flight in his own words. He uses quotation marks to show that these are Lindbergh's actual words.

Next Stop, Paris

Lindbergh's need for sleep vanished. Hope surged through his body. Minutes later, the *Spirit of St. Louis*'s motor started coughing ominously. Lindbergh prepared for a crash landing.

Then he realized one of the fuel tanks in the nose had run dry. He had forgotten to switch to his reserve tank. He turned a valve and the motor resumed its steady rhythm.

As the sun went down, Lindbergh crossed the English Channel into France. He had now flown 3,500 miles, breaking the world's distance record. For the first time he felt hungry. He gnawed on one of five sandwiches a friend had given him before takeoff. He could barely swallow each bite. His body was close to collapsing.

As Lindbergh neared Paris, he climbed to 4,000 feet. Below him he saw the lights of the city. He circled above the illuminated Eiffel Tower and after momentary confusion found Le Bourget Airport. He fastened his safety belt, cut his air speed and made a perfect landing in the middle of the runway. It was 10:24 P.M. Paris time—33$\frac{1}{2}$ hours since Lindbergh left New York.

Seconds later, reporters flashed the news of his landing around the world. In America people rushed into the street, cheering. At the airfield as many as 150,000 wildly excited French men and women were waiting for Lindbergh. The moment he cut his engine, they smashed down fences and stormed past policemen to greet him. They dragged him out of the plane and carried him around on their shoulders for several minutes. Some of them began tearing pieces off the plane for souvenirs.

French military fliers rescued Lindbergh and the *Spirit of St. Louis* from the excited crowd. They drove him to the American ambassador's house in Paris. There he ate, talked briefly to reporters, and asked permission to go to sleep. It was 4:30 A.M. He had been awake for 63 hours.

At 1 P.M. the next day, the former "flying fool" awoke to find himself the most famous man in the world. Calvin Coolidge, the president of the United States, had congratulated him by cablegram. The Prince of Wales had sent him a "well done." Newspapers in Rome, Bombay and Shanghai called him a hero. Twenty-five motion picture operators and 50 photographers wanted to take his picture. Two hundred reporters were begging for interviews.

Before he did anything else, Lindbergh insisted on calling his mother, Evangeline, in Detroit. He told her the trip over was "wonderful" and he was feeling fine. She told him to get plenty of rest. He had been under "a tremendous strain."[3]

Think Aloud

[3]*I think the way the text ends is interesting. Many important people wanted to talk to Lindbergh and congratulate him on his incredible flight, but the one person he wanted to talk to was his mother. I think this shows that he was a very down-to-earth and humble person.*

After Reading

Take Notes: Invite students to work in small groups to recall details from the story. Have them create a script for a radio broadcast that describes Lindbergh's historic flight from start to finish. Remind students to include descriptive details to help their listeners visualize the different things that happened on the journey.

Student Think Aloud

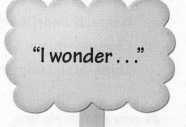

"I wonder . . ."

Use Copying Master number 1 to prompt students to share questions they had about Charles Lindbergh and his famous flight.

Cultural Perspective

Lindbergh returned to America on the *USS Memphis* as part of a convoy of warships and aircraft. Four million people lined the streets of New York for a parade in his honor. President Calvin Coolidge presented Lindbergh with the Congressional Medal of Honor, the nation's highest honor. Have students discuss the historical, social, and cultural aspects of this nonfiction piece from long ago.

Think and Respond

1. Why did people call Charles Lindbergh "The Flying Fool"? Do you think they still called him this after the flight? Why or why not? *Possible responses: They called him a fool because he was young, had little experience flying, and was making the flight by himself. No, I don't think they called him this after the flight. The author calls Lindbergh the former "flying fool" and treats him like a hero.* **Analytical**

2. Identify some specific facts about Lindbergh's flight across the Atlantic. How does this type of information add to the story? *Possible responses: The writer includes facts and figures about Lindbergh's landing in Paris. The specific details about his altitude, the time he landed, and the number of hours he flew are all facts that give readers more information about this event.* **Text Structure**

3. What makes this nonfiction story so interesting to read? What does the author want people to learn about Lindbergh's character? *Possible responses: It is about a man who is called a fool but ends up achieving something incredible. People learn that Lindbergh was very daring and courageous. They also learn that he was humble and polite.* **Author's Purpose**

Ant Jokes and Riddles

Genre: Humor/Jokes and Riddles

Comprehension Strategy: Generate Questions

Think-Aloud Copying Master number 1

Before Reading

Genre: Tell students they will listen to a series of jokes and riddles that all relate to ants. Ask students to give their own definitions of a joke and a riddle. Then explain that the writers of riddles think about the many different meanings a word can have. This allows them to play with words to create humor—using puns (the humorous usage of a word that involves two or more of its meanings), synonyms (words with similar meanings), homophones (words that sound the same but have different meanings and spellings), and idioms (expressions of speech). Explain that many times the double meaning of a riddle's answer is what makes a riddle funny.

Expand Vocabulary: To help students comprehend the puns in the riddles, introduce the following words before reading:

> *antique:* very old
>
> *antacid:* a medicine that soothes an upset stomach
>
> *tenants:* people who pay a landlord money so they can live in apartments or houses
>
> *dictator:* someone who rules with total control

Set a Purpose for Reading: Invite students to listen to the jokes and riddles to see what type of word play they can identify.

During Reading

Read each joke or riddle and pause to allow students to find the humor in it. Read through the jokes and riddles the first time without interruptions. Then reread, pausing to draw students' attention to the Think Alouds and genre note.

Ant Jokes and Riddles

What do you call a really big ant? *A gi-ant.*

What do you call a very old ant? Ant-ique.

What kind of ant carries a trunk around? *An eleph-ant.*

What game do ants and elephants play? *Squash.*[1]

What does an anteater take when it has an upset stomach? Ant-acid.

How does a bug get rid of bad breath? *It gargles with an ant-iseptic.*

Why was the farmer so upset? *He had ants in his plants.*

Which insects should you hire to build a house? *Carpenter ants.*

What crawls on the ground and wears uniforms and helmets? *Army ants.*

How many ants do you need to rent an apartment? Ten-ants.

Where do ants go to eat? *A restaur-ant.*

Why did the ant run really fast along the boxtop? *Because the box said "Tear Along Dotted Line."*

Why do ants dance on top of jars? *Because the lid says "Twist to Open."*

What did the scullery maid say to the lord of the manor when he asked why she kept the kitchen spotlessly clean? *"There's no ants, sir."*[2]

Knock, knock.
Who's there?
Ant.
Ant who?
Ant'cha glad you answered the door?

What do you call an ant that sets up little booths and sells things? *A merch-ant.*

Think Aloud

[1]*I know that squash is a vegetable, but the riddle asks about a game, so squash must also be the name of a game. I can picture in my mind a game between a huge elephant and a teeny, tiny ant. This makes me think of another meaning of the word squash: the verb meaning "to flatten or crush." That is exactly what might happen when an elephant and an ant try to play together!*

Think Aloud

[2]*At first I wondered why this was funny. Then I realized that when you say the words "There's no ants, sir," it sounds like you are saying, "There's no answer." The maid is literally saying that there are no ants in the spotless kitchen, but the riddle is she does not have an answer for the lord!*

What do you call an ant that works endlessly in the field for no pay? *A peas-ant.*

What do you call the leader of all the ants? *The presid-ant.*

What do you call an ant dictator? *A tyr-ant.*

What do you call an ant that skips school? *Tru-ant.*

What do you call an ant that writes letters? *A correspond-ant.*

What do you call an ant that moves to America? *An immigr-ant.*

What do you call an ant that is shipped to America? *Import-ant.*[3]

Where do ants go on vacation? *Frants.*

Which insect was a famous painter? *Rembr-ant.*

What do you call a newborn ant? *A baby buggy.*

What do you call a nicely dressed ant? *Eleg-ant.*

What do you call an ant that spends all kinds of money to get the biggest and the best of everything? *Extravag-ant.*

Why aren't ants smelly? *Deodor-ant.*

What do you call an ant that is good at keeping track of money? *An account-ant.*

What do you call all the children and grandchildren and great-grandchildren of an ant? *Its descend-ants.*

Which appetizer do bugs eat? *Ant-ipasto.*

After Reading

Set a Purpose for Rereading: Once students have enjoyed listening to the jokes just for fun, reread the selection and help them identify the different types of word play. Then have students work in small groups to write and share their own ant jokes and riddles.

Student Think Aloud

Use Copying Master number 1 to prompt students to discuss how specific jokes or riddles led them to ask questions about words that they did not understand.

"I wonder . . ."

Cultural Perspective

Many ancient documents from a variety of cultures include riddles. Riddles told orally probably date back to the beginning of language. The oldest known written riddle can be traced to a tablet produced by the Babylonian culture around 4,000 years ago.

Think and Respond

1. Identify some riddles in which the writer creates humor by using a word that has more than one meaning. What are some different meanings of the word? *Possible responses: What game do ants and elephants play?* Squash. Squash *is the name of a vegetable, the name of a game, and a verb that means "to crush." Why did the ant run really fast along the boxtop? Because the box said, "Tear Along Dotted Line."* Tear *is a verb that can mean "to rip open" or "to run really fast."* **Critical**

2. What makes a joke or riddle funny? *Possible response: The writer uses words creatively to make people laugh.* **Genre**

3. Why do the writers of jokes and riddles need to keep them simple and use topics known to most people? *Possible response: Simple ones are easier to figure out and remember. If people understand the topic, they will be able to understand what makes the joke or riddle funny.* **Author's Purpose**

Plays and Choral Readings

WHODUNIT?
WOO KNOWS . . .

by Anne M. Miranda

CAST:

Offstage Voice	Ms. Byrd
Ms. Woo	Mr. Lamb
Olivia Woo	Ms. Holstein
Manny the Parrot	Mr. Colt
Detective Billie	Mr. Boxer

SETTING:
A travel agency

PROLOGUE

[The stage is dark.]

SOUND EFFECTS: [footsteps; door being unlocked, opened, and shut; footsteps; safe door being unlocked, opened, closed, and locked; footsteps; chair scraping across a floor; jingling of keys; click of a switch; hum of a computer]

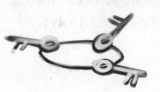

Offstage Voice: [soft whisper] Now, let's see what we've got here . . .

SOUND EFFECTS: [clicking of a computer keyboard]

Offstage Voice: [singing softly] Baa, baa, black sheep, have you any wool? Yes, sir, yes, sir, three bags full. . . .

ACT I

[Lights up]

Ms. Woo: Good morning, Olivia! How did you sleep? I made you some toast, and there's orange juice in the fridge.

Olivia: Thanks, Mom.

Ms. Woo: Well, now that the Memorial Day weekend is over, I've got a busy schedule for the next couple of months.

Olivia: I'm glad I'm on vacation!

Ms. Woo: Lucky you! Summer is a good time to slow down for most people, but not travel agents. We're still busy planning other people's vacations. Speaking of plans, what are you doing today?

Olivia: I really don't know, Mom. My detective business seems to be pretty slow these days—I wonder if it has anything to do with the hot weather we've been having. It's been a while since I've had any detecting to do.

Ms. Woo: So I've noticed.

Olivia: If it would be all right with you, maybe I'll spend the day at your office. I could help you out on the computer.

Ms. Woo: That would be great, Olivia.

SOUND EFFECTS: [thud of newspaper against the door]

Ms. Woo: That must be the newspaper.

Olivia: Don't get up, Mom. I'll get it.

SOUND EFFECTS: [door opening and closing, rustling of paper]

Ms. Woo: See anything interesting?

Olivia: I'll say! Just listen to this headline: QUADRUPLETS BORN AT MEMORIAL HOSPITAL. How about that? Four babies born on Memorial Day!

Ms. Woo: There must have been quite a bit of excitement at the hospital on that day! Anything else?

Olivia: Just the usual. . . . No, wait! You won't believe this! "MEMORIAL DAY BREAK-INS. Five homes in the area were burglarized over the Memorial Day weekend. According to the police, in each case the owners were on vacation.

The homeowners were contacted and have given permission for their names to be released. The burglary victims are: James and Carol Janson, 35 Maple Street; Victoria Temple, 249 Oak Street; Lisa and Jeff Campo, 19 Washington Avenue; Buzz Saw, 119 West Main Street; Keesha and Ben Owens, 310 Lincoln Drive."

Ms. Woo: Hmmm. . . . Those names certainly sound familiar. Let me see that paper a minute, will you?

Olivia: Are any of them your clients?

Ms. Woo: I think almost all of them are—everyone except Buzz Saw, that is. I've never heard of him.

Olivia: Mom, don't you remember? Buzz Saw is that rock star I told you about—the one who just moved into town. His real name is Bob Jones.

Ms. Woo: Bob Jones? Now let me think. . . . Of course! I remember now. His secretary called me last week and had me book airline tickets for him using his real name. He must like to travel incognito. I just never made the connection.

Olivia: That means that all these people are your clients.

Ms. Woo: You're right. What a coincidence!

Olivia: I'd say it's more than just a coincidence, Mom—it's downright suspicious. We'd better go over to the office and check your files right away.

Ms. Woo: I hate to say it, Olivia, but this may turn out to be that mystery you were hoping for. Let's get moving.

SOUND EFFECTS: [traffic sounds, footsteps]

Olivia: Well, Mom, the office door hasn't been forced, and there are no broken windows.

SOUND EFFECTS: [key turning in lock, door opening and closing]

Manny: Squawk. Good morning, good morning. Can I help you?

Olivia: I wish you could, Manny! Yes, sir, do I ever!

Manny: Squawk! Baa, baa, black sheep, have you any wool? Yes, sir! Yes, sir! Three bags full. Squawk!

Olivia: Hey, Manny, you've learned a new song. I've never heard you sing that one before. I wonder who taught it to you.

Ms. Woo: Well, this is reassuring. Everything seems to be just as I left it on Friday.

Olivia: What about your disks? Are there any missing?

Ms. Woo: I keep the disks in the safe with the tickets. Here's the key to the safe. Go ahead and check.

Olivia: Okay, I've got it open. What disks am I looking for?

Ms. Woo: Look for the one with last week's dates on the label.

Olivia: Here it is—May 25th to May 31st. Safe and sound. Let's check the names against the list in the paper.

Ms. Woo: Okay, just let me unlock the computer and we'll see.

SOUND EFFECTS: [chair scraping across a floor, jingling of keys, click of a switch, hum of a computer, clicking of a computer keyboard]

Ms. Woo: Hmmm. . . . Well, there's no doubt about it. All the names in the paper are on this disk. They're my clients, all right. Those people all left on their vacations last week, and I made their travel plans.

Olivia: Did you book them on the same airline by any chance?

Ms. Woo: Unfortunately not. They all had different destinations, flew on different airlines, and left on different days. I'm afraid there's absolutely no connection there.

Olivia: Then the only way the Memorial Day Burglar could have gotten all those names was from your files.

Ms. Woo: It certainly looks that way. I'm calling the police this minute.

SOUND EFFECTS: [dialing telephone]

Ms. Woo: Hello? May I speak with Detective Billie, please? This is Ms. Woo of the Paradise Travel Agency. . . . What? He's on his way here now? I see. Thank you.

Olivia: Mom, surely Detective Billie doesn't suspect you!

Ms. Woo: Well, he may not suspect me. But by talking to each of the burglary victims, he has probably figured out that I do have the information about everyone's vacation.

Olivia: But there must be a way someone else could have gotten access to this information.

Ms. Woo: There's only one way that I can think of.

Olivia: And that's by copying that disk!

Ms. Woo: The trouble is, I don't see how. To keep something like this from happening, I always store the disks in the safe, and I always lock my computer when I leave the office. I'm the only one who has those two keys.

Olivia: Right, and don't forget, when we arrived this morning, the door to the office was locked as usual.

SOUND EFFECTS: [knock at the door, door opening and closing]

Detective Billie: Good morning, Ms. Woo. Hi, Olivia. I heard on my car radio that you had called the station, so I guess you've probably figured out why I'm here. I must say it's a big help to have "Whodunit" Woo right on the scene.

Olivia: Thanks, Detective Billie.

Manny: Old MacDonald had a farm, E-I-E-I-O. Squawk! And on his farm, he had a goat, E-I-E-I-O!

Detective Billie: Good morning, Manny. And thanks a lot!

Olivia: Oh, I apologize for Manny, Detective Billie. He doesn't mean to be insulting. He sings that song to everyone.

Detective Billie: It's okay. Now, tell me, what have you found here?

Olivia: Well, Detective Billie, when we realized all the robbery victims were Mom's clients, we rushed over here to see if any of Mom's files had been stolen. But number one, no one had broken into the office. Number two, the computer disk that has all the data on the burglary victims' travel plans was still locked in the safe. And number three, even if someone had managed to get hold of the disk, he or she couldn't have copied it because Mom's computer was locked. And here are her keys—which she had all weekend—so they weren't lost or stolen.

SOUND EFFECTS: [jangling of keys]

Detective Billie: Hmmm. I'd say the keys are definitely the key to this mystery. The office key and the keys to the computer and the safe must have been copied. May I see them, please?

Olivia: Here they are. Wait! Look at that! That orange stuff looks like wax!

Detective Billie: That, my young detective, is just what we're looking for. That wax is the very kind that's used for making impressions of keys.

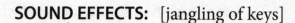

Olivia: Now we're getting somewhere!

SOUND EFFECTS: [telephone ringing]

Ms. Woo: Paradise Travel Agency. May I help you? Yes . . . yes, he's here. It's for you, Detective.

Detective Billie: Billie here. What's up? Uh-huh. Okay, I'll be there in fifteen minutes.

SOUND EFFECTS: [telephone receiver being replaced]

Detective Billie: I'm sorry; something urgent has just come up. I've got to go, but I'll be back later so we can continue our discussion.

Ms. Woo: All right. We'll be here.

SOUND EFFECTS: [door opening and closing]

Olivia: Mom, I don't think Detective Billie suspects you of being involved, but I'd like to figure this out. Let's start with the keys. The burglaries didn't occur until the weekend, even though some of your clients left on vacation several days before that. That means the burglar probably didn't have the keys until Friday. So the burglar was probably here on Friday, and . . .

Ms. Woo: And what?

Olivia: And since you never leave your keys lying around, you probably gave the burglar the keys for some seemingly innocent reason. Let's start with who was here Friday.

Ms. Woo: Here's my appointment book. Let's see, at 10:15, Ms. Holstein came in to plan her vacation. At noon, Mr. Boxer came to pick up my car for repairs. At 1:30, Mr. Colt came in to talk about his vacation. At 2:30, Mr. Lamb came in to pick up some travel brochures. And at 5:30, Ms. Byrd came in to clean the office.

Olivia: So there were five people in the office on Friday. Do you remember if anyone borrowed your keys?

Ms. Woo: Well, Ms. Byrd always uses the keys to open the supply closet when she comes in to clean.

Olivia: That's one.

Ms. Woo: Now, Olivia, you know that Ms. Byrd is as honest as the day is long.

Olivia: I agree, but I'm sure the police will say that anyone who had access to those keys is a suspect. How about the others?

Ms. Woo: Well, Mr. Boxer from the garage came to check the rattle I noticed in the engine. He took the keys so that he could take the car for a test drive around the block.

Olivia: That's two.

Ms. Woo: Hmmm. . . . Ms. Holstein used the lavatory key while she was here— and Mr. Lamb used the lavatory key, too!

Olivia: That's four! Everyone had the keys except Mr. Colt.

Ms. Woo: Wait a minute! Mr. Boxer had to rush off for some unexplained reason. So when he saw Mr. Colt coming in, he gave Mr. Colt the keys to return to me.

Olivia: That's five out of five! Everyone who was in here on Friday had your keys at one time or another.

Ms. Woo: Olivia, some of those people are coming in again today.

Olivia: What luck! Maybe we can do some detective work on our own before Detective Billie gets back.

Ms. Woo: Just what do you have in mind?

Olivia: Well, one thing we know is that the Memorial Day Burglar knows how to operate your computer. If we can find out who among those five people knows how to run a computer like yours, that would be a big clue.

Ms. Woo: That's a great idea, but how will we find out?

Olivia: I'm a kid. They'll never be suspicious of me. I'll get them talking about computers and act as if I don't know much about them. I think they'll swallow it.

Manny: There was an old lady, who swallowed a fly. I don't know why she swallowed a fly!

Olivia: Too bad Manny can't tell us. I'll bet he knows.

ACT II

SOUND EFFECTS: [knock on the door, door opening and closing, footsteps]

Olivia: Hello, Ms. Byrd. You look chipper this morning!

Manny: Old MacDonald had a farm, E-I-E-I-O. Squawk! And on his farm, he had a chicken, E-I-E-I-O!

Ms. Byrd: That Manny! He's the smartest parrot! He and I talk all the time. Sometimes I even teach him a song.

Olivia: Oh, really? He's just learned a new tune. You didn't happen to teach him "Baa, Baa, Black Sheep," by any chance?

Ms. Byrd: No, but I once taught him how to sing "Kookaburra." He learned it in no time. Well, I came by to get my pay.

Ms. Woo: Of course, Ms. Byrd. Why don't you take a seat while I write out a check.

Ms. Byrd: Thanks. I'll perch right here.

Baa Baa Black Sheep

Olivia: When you were here on Friday afternoon, did you find a game disk lying around?

Ms. Byrd: What's a game disk?

Olivia: A computer disk. You know, a little, square, black, plastic thing with a hole in the middle.

Ms. Byrd: Your mother never leaves anything out. Why don't you look in that box on the desk. I think that's where she keeps those things when she's working at her computer.

SOUND EFFECTS: [door opening and closing]

Ms. Woo: Good morning, Mr. Lamb.

Manny: Old MacDonald had a farm, E-I-E-I-O. Squawk! And on his farm, he had a sheep, E-I-E-I-O!

Ms. Woo: That's enough, Manny. I didn't expect to see you today, Mr. Lamb. Did you decide to go to Sheepshead Bay?

Mr. Lamb: Actually, I've changed my mind. I've decided to take that around-the-world cruise I've always dreamed of. This would be a good time for me to go. Do you think you can arrange it? I'd like to leave as soon as possible.

Ms. Woo: An around-the-world cruise? Lucky you, Mr. Lamb! We can begin planning it just as soon as I finish with Ms. Byrd.

Ms. Byrd: Oh, I'm in no hurry. Go ahead and help Mr. Lamb. I'll just feed Manny and change his water while I'm waiting.

Ms. Woo: Thank you, Ms. Byrd. . . . Oh, dear, the reservations computer is down. There's a message saying that full service should be restored in a few minutes. Mr. Lamb, I'm afraid we'll just have to wait for a bit.

SOUND EFFECTS: [door opening and closing]

Olivia: Good morning, Ms. Holstein. Nice day, isn't it?

Manny: Old MacDonald had a farm, E-I-E-I-O. Squawk! And on his farm, he had a cow, E-I-E-I-O!

Ms. Holstein: Who taught that bird to sing that utterly ridiculous song?

Olivia: I'm sorry, Ms. Holstein. How may we help you?

Ms. Holstein: I just dropped in to pick up my tickets. I'm leaving for my vacation tomorrow. I'm so excited.

Mr. Lamb: Ah, Bermuda—pink sand and sunny skies!

Ms. Byrd: Oh, yes, I hear Bermuda is beautiful this time of year.

Olivia: Wow! Ms. Holstein, excuse me for interrupting, but does that new red sports car out in front belong to you?

Ms. Holstein: Yes, isn't it a beauty? I just came into some unexpected cash, and I decided to give myself a special treat. Now, are my tickets ready?

Ms. Woo: Your tickets are ready, but I'd like to double-check your seat assignment. Could you wait just a few minutes? The reservations computer is temporarily down.

Ms. Holstein: The computer is down? What does that mean?

Mr. Lamb: Ms. Woo gets information about reservations from a central computer, and sometimes things go wrong with the equipment. It's usually just a short wait until they clear up the problem.

Olivia: I know I've seen you using a computer at the library, Ms. Holstein. Isn't it like my mother's?

Ms. Holstein: Oh, no, we have different computers, and we use different software. I must confess I'm just becoming computer literate—the library system is the only one I know.

Mr. Colt: Knock, knock, anybody here? Howdy, y'all!

Ms. Woo: Hello, Mr. Colt. Pull up a chair.

Manny: Old MacDonald had a farm, E-I-E-I-O. Squawk! And on his farm, he had a horse, E-I-E-I-O!

Mr. Colt: I wish Manny knew a nice Western song like "Home, Home on the Range." I'd teach it to him myself, but I can't carry a tune in a bucket. Well, enough about music. I'm here to pick up some tickets.

Ms. Holstein: Oh, are you going on vacation, too?

Mr. Colt: Yup, and I can't wait! Sagebrush! Tumbleweeds! Wide open spaces!

Mr. Lamb: Ah, yes, Texas, the Lone Star State. Have you . . .

Mr. Boxer: Excuse me, the door was open. Hello, all. Hi, Manny.

Manny: Old MacDonald had a farm, E-I-E-I-O. Squawk! And on his farm, he had a dog, E-I-E-I-O!

Ms. Woo: Mr. Boxer! I have a bone to pick with you. You didn't fix my car on Friday.

Mr. Boxer: I knew I'd be in the doghouse. You see, Ms. Woo, your car didn't have a serious problem, and I was really worried about my wife. So I rushed home. Just in time, too. I took her right to the hospital.

Ms. Woo: Goodness! Was she hurt? Is it serious?

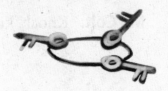

Mr. Boxer: No, no, everything is great! My wife had quadruplets on Memorial Day! Two girls and two boys—everybody's doing just fine, thank you.

Olivia: Oh, wow! We read the headline in the paper just this morning, but we didn't realize it was about you.

Ms. Woo: And your wife, too, of course!

All: Congratulations!

Ms. Byrd: Raising four children can be pretty expensive.

Mr. Boxer: True, but we'll manage. Say, what's that flickering?

Ms. Woo: Oh, the fluorescent light bulb is about to go out. I'll just go downstairs and get the ladder and a new bulb.

SOUND EFFECTS: [footsteps, door opening]

Mr. Colt: If that's my disk in the machine, I can check to see if my flight has been booked.

Mr. Lamb: First, you'll have to bring up your file. Ms. Woo was working on mine.

Olivia: You may have to wait, Mr. Colt. The central reservations computer is down. Of course, it may be fixed by now, but I don't know how to find out.

Mr. Colt: Let me try. They don't call me "Hacker" for nothing.

Mr. Boxer: Maybe I can help you. We use the same computer down at the garage.

Ms. Woo: I'm back. Sorry I took so long, but I had to find a screwdriver. What's everyone doing at my computer?

Olivia: It's okay, Mom. We're just trying to find out if the central computer has come back up again.

Ms. Woo: I'll take care of it. But first I have to fix that flickering light. It will only take me a minute.

Mr. Lamb: Can I help, Ms. Woo? I'm real handy—there's nothing mechanical or electrical that I can't fix. I'll have that bulb changed in two shakes of a lamb's tail!

Ms. Woo: Thanks, Mr. Lamb. I'll just get back to that computer.

SOUND EFFECTS: [clanking of tools]

Mr. Lamb: [singing softly] Baa, baa, black sheep, have you any wool?

Mr. Colt: Maybe I'd better come back later.

Mr. Boxer: Do you need a lift? I'm going downtown.

Mr. Lamb: [singing softly] Yes, sir, yes, sir, three bags full.

Ms. Woo: I'm sorry to keep you waiting so long, Ms. Byrd.

Mr. Lamb: [singing softly] One for my master, one for my dame.

Ms. Byrd: No problem, Ms. Woo. I'm enjoying myself.

SOUND EFFECTS: [door opening and closing]

Detective Billie: I'm back, Ms. Woo. Ahem! May I have your attention please! This office is being investigated in connection with the Memorial Day burglaries. I'll have to ask everyone to leave now.

Ms. Byrd and Mr. Lamb: Under investigation?

Mr. Colt and Ms. Holstein: Burglaries?

Mr. Boxer: Good grief!

Olivia: Excuse me, Detective Billie. The Memorial Day Burglar is in this room right now. I'm sure of it.

Ms. Holstein: It's best to leave police work to the police, young lady.

Detective Billie: I'll handle this, ma'am. That's a serious accusation, Olivia. What evidence do you have?

Olivia: The Memorial Day Burglar copied my mother's client files from her disk. That's how the thief found out which houses would be empty over the weekend, right?

Detective Billie: That sounds plausible. Go on.

Olivia: As you said, it's a question of keys. Ms. Byrd uses Mom's keys every week when she cleans the office. She could easily have made wax impressions of them. But Ms. Byrd has worked for my mother for a long time and has never taken so much as a paper clip. Besides, Ms. Byrd knows absolutely nothing about computers.

Ms. Byrd: She's right. I don't know a thing about computers.

Olivia: Ms. Holstein has just come into a lot of money. See her expensive new car outside? Also, she borrowed the keys on Friday to use the lavatory. She does use a computer at the library, but she doesn't know anything about my mother's software program. The thief would have to know about that program to get the computer to run and to copy the disk.

Ms. Holstein: That's right. I don't know anything about her mother's computer.

Olivia: Which brings us to Mr. Boxer. Mr. Boxer took the keys on Friday to give Mom's car a test drive around the block. He also knows a lot about computers. In fact, he has an identical machine at the garage. Also, as Ms. Byrd pointed out, Mr. Boxer certainly needs money just now.

Mr. Boxer: But I was at the hospital from Friday afternoon through Tuesday night.

Olivia: Yes, I think all of us would agree that Mr. Boxer has an unshakable alibi for the Memorial Day weekend.

Detective Billie: All right, who's next?

Olivia: Well, Mr. Boxer asked Mr. Colt to return my mom's keys to her, so Mr. Colt could have made an impression of them. What's more, his nickname is "Hacker." A hacker is someone who can do almost anything with a computer.

Detective Billie: Then he could have gotten the names of all those people who were robbed.

Olivia: Right.

Detective Billie: Sounds suspicious to me!

Olivia: I'm not so sure that Mr. Colt is your man, though. Don't forget, Mr. Lamb had Mom's keys last Friday when he borrowed them to use the lavatory. He also knows a lot about computers. And when he came in today, he wanted to change his plans from a weekend trip to an around-the-world cruise. That takes a lot of money.

Detective Billie: But that's not real evidence.

Olivia: True. But how did he know Ms. Holstein was going to Bermuda? And that Mr. Colt was going to Texas?

Mr. Lamb: I guessed. I'm good at putting two and two together.

Detective Billie: Well, Olivia, you may not have solved the case, but at least you've narrowed the number of suspects down to two—Mr. Colt and Mr. Lamb. Now if you two gentlemen would kindly accompany me to the station for further questioning . . .

Olivia: I don't think that will be necessary, Detective Billie. You see, the thief has to be able to sing.

Detective Billie: Excuse me? What does singing have to do with it?

Olivia: When Mom and I arrived at the office this morning, Manny was singing a song that we had never heard him sing before. Mom was here until late on Friday. That means Manny must have learned that song between Friday night and Monday night—a period when the office was closed.

Detective Billie: I follow you.

Olivia: Just now, Mr. Lamb sang the very same song while he was changing the light bulb. My theory is that Mr. Lamb is in the habit of humming or singing while he works. I think he was singing "Baa, Baa, Black Sheep" when he was here copying Mom's files.

Mr. Lamb: More guesswork. Ridiculous!

Olivia: And, finally, Mr. Lamb is very handy. He said so himself. If you search his workshop, I'm sure you'll find the wax he used to make the impressions of Mom's keys plus a machine that makes duplicate keys.

Mr. Lamb: Drat that junior detective and her feathered friend!

Detective Billie: Okay, let's go quietly, Mr. Lamb. Thanks, "Whodunit" Woo, you've done it again!

Ms. Woo: Olivia, you're terrific!

Olivia: Thanks, Mom. Mr. Lamb turned out to be a real wolf in sheep's clothing. Oh, and let's not forget to thank Manny. Without him, I never would have cracked this case.

Manny: Baa, baa, black sheep, have you any wool? Yes, sir, yes, sir, three bags full. One for my master, one for my dame, And one for the naughty crook who won't steal again! Squawk! Squawk!

Baa Baa
Black Sheep

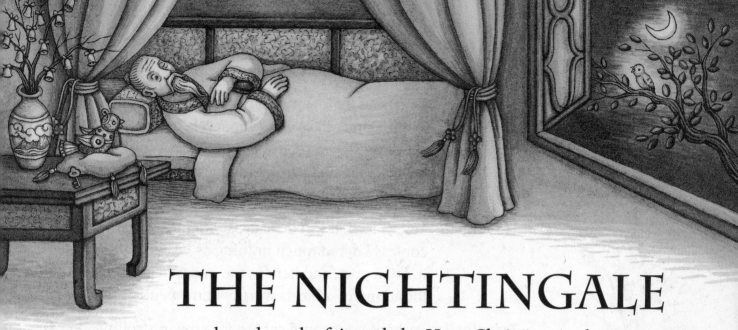

THE NIGHTINGALE

based on the fairy tale by Hans Christian Andersen

by Kathleen M. Fischer

CAST:

Narrator	Emperor	Lady 2
Traveler 1	Empress	Messenger
Traveler 2	Chamberlain	Jeweled Bird
Gardener	Courtier 1	Music Master
Nightingale	Courtier 2	Watchmaker
Fisherman	Kitchen Maid	
Fisherman's Wife	Lady 1	

SETTING:

Ancient China

Narrator: The story of the nightingale happened in China many years ago. But that's all the more reason for telling it today, so that its lesson won't be forgotten. In those days, the emperor of China was a very powerful and wealthy ruler. His palace was the most beautiful in all the world. In fact, it was so extraordinary that travelers came from round the world to gaze at its wonders for themselves.

Traveler 1: Greetings, fellow traveler! I've journeyed to distant lands in search of marvels to write about, yet never have I seen such splendor. Who would believe that a palace could be made of fine porcelain?

Traveler 2: Yes, indeed. It's so delicate, so fragile, I must confess I dared touch nothing as I walked through it. I'm a poet, and here in the imperial palace I've found many subjects worthy of my pen.

Traveler 1: Perhaps you would care to join me in strolling through the emperor's magnificent gardens.

Traveler 2: Nothing would please me more. Ah, look there. The gardener is tying bells to those flowers. How odd!

Traveler 1: Most unusual! We must find out why. . . . Forgive us for interrupting your labors, Imperial Gardener. We are visitors to your kingdom and are seeking to understand your customs. Tell us, please, why are you hanging bells on these flowers?

Gardener: You see, honored travelers, only the rarest and most exquisite flowers are allowed to grow in the emperor's garden. It is my imperial duty to select the loveliest blossoms and tie little silver bells to them, so that passersby will be sure to admire them.

Traveler 2: We congratulate you on such an ingenious plan. Incidentally, just how large are the emperor's gardens?

Gardener: How large? Why, they're so large that even I don't know where they end! However, I do know that if you walk far enough, you'll come to an immense forest that extends to the edge of the sea.

Narrator: The next day, the two travelers set forth on a journey to learn the extent of the emperor's gardens. As they walked through the forest, they marveled at the beautiful things they heard and saw.

Traveler 2: Just listen to those wonderful sounds: the chirping of the insects, the sighing of the wind in the trees, the babbling of the brook. The sound of the silver bells in the imperial gardens is sweet, yet these sounds are sweeter still.

Traveler 1: Yes, and just look at those colors: the different hues of the leaves and all the shades of blue in the sky. The gilded porcelain in the emperor's palace is wonderful to behold, yet the colors in the forest are lovelier still.

Narrator: The two travelers continued on their way until they reached the sea, where the tall trees stretched their branches over the deep blue water. Standing under one of the trees, they heard a most glorious sound.

Nightingale: [song of the nightingale]

Narrator: At that moment, a fisherman and his wife happened by on their way to the sea to tend their nets.

Traveler 1: Good day to you both.

Fisherman: Good day, sir.

Traveler 2: Can you tell us—what is that sound we hear?

Fisherman: That, sir, is the nightingale who lives in this forest.

Wife: Her song is beautiful, don't you agree?

Traveler 2: Ah, yes. I would say that in this kingdom of beautiful things, it's the loveliest of all!

Traveler 1: You're right, my friend. When I get home, I shall write books describing all the amazing things I've seen. But the place of honor will surely go to the nightingale.

Traveler 2: And I shall write exquisite poems about the nightingale who lives in the forest by the deep blue sea.

Narrator: In time, these travelers' books and poems went all over the world. Eventually, some of them reached the emperor himself! He sat on his golden throne reading and nodding his head over the glowing descriptions of his palace and its grounds.

Emperor: Ah, yes, this writer says the porcelain in my palace cannot be matched anywhere in the world.

Empress: How true, my husband, how true. And this poet mentions that the palace seems to glow like a million fireflies when it is lit by lantern light.

Emperor: As indeed it does! But what's this? This writer says, "The nightingale is the loveliest thing of all." What nightingale? No one has ever told me of any nightingale! Instead, I have to read about her in a book! Courtier, send my chamberlain to me immediately.

Narrator: The chamberlain was the emperor's gentleman-in-waiting. He was so grand that if anyone of lower rank spoke to him, he only answered "Peh!"—which means nothing at all.

Chamberlain: You wished to see me, Your Imperial Majesty?

Emperor: I have just read in this very learned book that a remarkable bird called a nightingale lives in my garden. Why haven't you told me about her?

Chamberlain: Nightingale, Your Majesty? I've never heard that name. I'm sure she has never been presented at court.

Emperor: Well, I command you to bring her here to sing for me tonight. Imagine, the whole world knows that I possess this marvel, yet I know nothing of her!

Chamberlain: This is the first time I've heard of her. But if she exists, she shall be found and brought to you.

Narrator: The chamberlain had no idea where to begin looking. He ran upstairs and then downstairs. He ran through all the rooms and corridors of the palace, asking all he met if they had heard of the nightingale. But no one had.

Chamberlain: Your Majesty, the story of the nightingale must have been invented by the writer. Perhaps you should not believe everything you read. Much of it is made up for people's entertainment.

Emperor: But I read it in a book sent to me by the mighty emperor of Japan. Therefore, it must be true! I insist on hearing the nightingale sing this very evening! If she does not appear, every courtier shall be held responsible!

Narrator: Again, the chamberlain ran upstairs and downstairs and through all the rooms and corridors. This time, half the court went with him, for no one wanted to be held responsible by the emperor! They asked everyone about the nightingale. To their dismay, it seemed that the bird was known the world over—except to the people at court! At last they came to the imperial kitchen, where they found a young kitchen maid scrubbing the pots.

Courtier 1: We've been all over the palace seeking information about a nightingale who is said to live in the imperial gardens.

Courtier 2: Do you know anything about such a bird?

Kitchen Maid: Yes, indeed; I know the nightingale. Every evening, I'm allowed to take table scraps to my sick mother, who lives near the sea. As I walk through the forest, I often hear the nightingale. Her song is so lovely it brings tears to my eyes.

Chamberlain: Little kitchen maid, if you lead us to the nightingale, I, personally, will see to it that you are given a permanent place in the imperial kitchen. Furthermore, you will be allowed to watch the emperor dine!

Narrator: So the kitchen maid, the chamberlain, and half the court set out for the forest where the nightingale lived. As they walked, they paused to admire the sights and sounds of the forest. Its wild beauty was so different from the manicured perfection that surrounded them at the palace. When they had gone some distance, they heard a cow mooing.

Lady 1: Ah, there she is!

Lady 2: My, my, what a strong voice for such a small creature!

Courtier 2: That's strange! I'm sure I've heard her before.

Kitchen Maid: Why, that's not the nightingale. It's only a cow mooing. We still have a long way to go.

Narrator: Then they heard some frogs croaking in a pond.

Courtier 1: Listen! There she is!

Lady 1: Lovely! Her voice is like little bells.

Kitchen Maid: No, those are frogs you hear. But it won't be long now.

Nightingale: [song of the nightingale]

Kitchen Maid: There, that's the nightingale! She's on that branch.

Chamberlain: Really? I never pictured her so . . . well . . . so small and gray and ordinary. Ah, well, perhaps being surrounded by so many distinguished members of the imperial court has caused her color to fade away.

Kitchen Maid: Little Nightingale, our gracious emperor would like to hear you sing.

Nightingale: It would be my pleasure.

Chamberlain: Most excellent singer, I have the honor to command you to appear at court this evening. There you will entertain His Imperial Majesty with your enchanting song.

Nightingale: My song sounds best out in the open; here the music is free to go wherever the breezes may carry it. But since the emperor wishes it, I will accompany you to the palace.

Narrator: At the palace, everything was scrubbed and polished for the occasion. Flowers hung with tiny bells were placed in all the corridors. With all the comings and goings, the bells jingled and jangled so that the people had to shout to be heard.

Emperor: Is everything ready? Where's the golden perch for the nightingale?

Empress: Why, it's been placed beside your golden throne.

Emperor: Good. Let the court enter.

Narrator: The entire court, dressed in their finest robes, assembled to hear the nightingale. Even the little kitchen maid, now assistant to the imperial cook, listened from the doorway. All eyes were on the nightingale. When the emperor nodded his head, the little gray bird began to sing.

Nightingale: [song of the nightingale]

Narrator: She sang so beautifully that tears came to the emperor's eyes and rolled down his cheeks.

Emperor: Little Nightingale, you have melted my heart. You shall have my golden slipper to wear around your neck.

Nightingale: Thank you, but Your Majesty has rewarded me enough. I've seen the tears in your eyes, and nothing could be more precious to me.

Narrator: And with that, the nightingale began to sing again. What a success she was! From that day on, she was compelled to remain at court. In addition to her golden perch, she had a golden cage of her very own. And twice each day and once each night she was allowed to go out, accompanied by twelve servants. Each servant held a silk ribbon attached to the nightingale's legs.

Nightingale: The emperor is kind and generous, for my golden cage is surely worth a fortune. Yet to a wild creature, a golden cage is but a gilded cell, and my twelve servants might as well be twelve prison guards. How I long for the freedom of the forest!

Narrator: Life went on this way until one day a large parcel arrived at the palace. The word "Nightingale" was carefully written on the outside.

Messenger: Your Imperial Majesty, I bring you this gift from the emperor of Japan.

Emperor: Perhaps it's another book about my famous nightingale. Here, let me open it.

Narrator: But it wasn't a book at all. There, lying in a velvet case, was a mechanical nightingale. It looked exactly like a real bird, but instead of feathers it was covered with gold and silver studded with diamonds, rubies, and sapphires. The entire court let out a single gasp of amazement and pleasure.

Chamberlain: Here is the key, Your Majesty. If you please, I will wind it up.

Jeweled Bird: [mechanical bird song]

Empress: How lovely! It's singing one of the nightingale's songs.

Lady 2: See how its tail moves up and down as it sings.

Emperor: What a thoughtful gift. Where is the messenger who brought it?

Messenger: Here I am, Your Royal Majesty.

Emperor: For your part in bringing me this gift, I bestow upon you the title of Chief Imperial Nightingale-Bringer. Now, let's hear both nightingales sing together.

Empress: Yes! What a duet that will be!

Narrator: So the two birds sang together, but the duet was not a success. The real nightingale sang freely in her own way, while the mechanical bird sang like clockwork.

Emperor: Music Master, the birds don't sing well together. Can you explain why that is so?

Music Master: The new bird is certainly not at fault, Your Majesty. It keeps absolutely perfect time. What's more, it sings as if I had taught it myself.

Narrator: So after that, the jeweled bird sang by itself. It was just as popular with the court as the real bird. Besides, it was much prettier to look at.

Jeweled Bird: [mechanical bird song]

Narrator: It sang its one and only song over and over again—thirty-three times by the chamberlain's count—without tiring. While everyone nodded their heads in time to the song, the real nightingale flew unnoticed to the window.

Nightingale: I will give up my place to the jeweled bird. Since it is not a living thing, it will not mind a gilded cage. And its song will sound the same no matter where it is. As for me, I will return to the freedom of my forest home.

Narrator: With that, the nightingale flew away from the porcelain palace, away from the golden cage, and away from the twelve servants with silk ribbons. Just then, the emperor recalled the other songster.

Emperor: Now it's time for my real nightingale to sing. Nightingale! Nightingale? Where is she?

Chamberlain: Why, she's gone! She must have flown out the open window.

Empress: The ungrateful bird!

Courtier 1: And after all the favors she has received here at court!

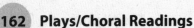

Chamberlain: Fortunately, you still have the better bird, Your Majesty.

Music Master: The chamberlain is right, Your Imperial Majesty. You see, with the real nightingale, you never know what you will hear. But with the mechanical bird, everything has been set beforehand. With this bird, there are no surprises; you always know exactly what it will sing.

Entire Court: Yes, yes, you're so right!

Narrator: The next day, the emperor commanded the music master to display the mechanical bird to the public. The fisherman and his wife were in the crowd.

Wife: It certainly looks very pretty. And it sounds . . . well . . . almost like the real nightingale.

Fisherman: You're right, wife, it is a good imitation. Still, something is missing. Unlike this mechanical bird, I never knew exactly how the nightingale would sound. There was always something fresh and surprising in her song. Despite the mechanical bird's beauty, I prefer the drab little nightingale's song.

Narrator: But the opinion of the fisherman carried no weight, and soon after the arrival of the mechanical bird, the emperor banished the real nightingale from his empire. He kept the jeweled bird on a silk cushion by his bed and raised its title to Chief Imperial Bedside-Singer. A year passed. Then one evening, as the emperor sat listening to the bird, something terrible happened.

Jeweled Bird: [mechanical bird song, followed by R-R-R-R-r-r-r- . . .]

Emperor: What's wrong?

Empress: Something cracked!

Chamberlain: Something snapped!

Emperor: Send for the court physician immediately!

Narrator: The court physician could do nothing, so the Imperial Watchmaker was summoned. After a lengthy examination and a great deal of painstaking labor, he was able to get the bird to work again.

Watchmaker: I have managed to repair the mechanism, Your Imperial Majesty, but the cogs are worn and cannot be replaced. The jeweled bird will sing, but its song will never sound exactly the same as it once did. Furthermore, I must regretfully suggest that it mustn't be wound too often. To protect the mechanism, I recommend that it be allowed to sing only once a year.

Emperor: Only once a year! Well, if it must be, it must be. It is still the finest songbird in my empire.

Narrator: Five years passed, and in all that time the jeweled bird sang only five times. But even then, it was almost too much of a strain. At the end of that time, a great sadness fell on the land. The emperor grew so ill it was said he would not live. People stood in the street, waiting to hear about his condition. When they asked the chamberlain, he only shook his head.

Chamberlain: Things look very grave indeed for the emperor.

Narrator: A new emperor was chosen, and all the court hastened to pay their respects to him.

Meanwhile, the old emperor lay alone in his magnificent bed hung with velvet curtains and golden tassels. Through an open window, the moon shone down on him and the jeweled bird at his bedside.

Emperor: I feel so cold and alone. . . . Music! I need music to cheer me. Little golden bird, I implore you; sing to me. I have given you precious stones and have even hung my golden slipper around your neck. Sing! Sing!

Narrator: But with no one to wind it up, the bird was silent. Suddenly, the sound of a beautiful song floated through the emperor's open window.

Nightingale: [song of the nightingale]

Emperor: Nightingale? Nightingale, is that really you?

Nightingale: Yes, I heard of your illness and came to bring you hope and joy.

Emperor: Oh, Nightingale, thank you! I banished you, yet you have come back to comfort me. How can I ever repay you?

Nightingale: You have already done that with the tears you shed the first time I sang to you. Tears are the jewels that gladden a singer's heart. But rest now. I'll sing you to sleep, and you'll awaken strong and healthy.

Narrator: When the emperor awoke, he felt refreshed and well. The sun was shining, and the faithful nightingale was still singing outside his window.

Emperor: Dear Nightingale, you must stay with me forever. You may sing whatever and whenever you wish, and I shall break the mechanical bird into a thousand pieces!

Nightingale: Oh no, Your Majesty, don't do that. The jeweled bird did the very best it could, and it will always be beautiful to look at. Keep it beside you in its accustomed place. As for me, to sing my best, I must live in the forest with the sky as my roof and a nest as my home. But I promise to come every evening of my own free will. I will sit on the branch outside your window and sing to you.

Emperor: I see I have been wrong, my friend. You have taught me that a wild creature should not be caged. From now on, it shall be as you wish. You shall be free to come and go as you please.

Narrator: Just then, the courtiers came tiptoeing into the royal bedchamber, expecting to find the emperor close to death.

Chamberlain: Shhh. Be very quiet, everyone.

Emperor: Good morning to you all!

Courtier 1: You're . . . You're . . . up!

Courtier 2: You're . . . You're . . . well!

Chamberlain: Your . . . Your . . . Your Majesty!

Narrator: From then on, the nightingale returned every evening to sing for the emperor, who lived to rule wisely for many years to come.

Nat Love, Western Hero

by Judith Bauer Stamper

CAST:
First Narrator
Second Narrator
Nat Love
Mrs. Love
Mr. Williams
Young Girl
Trail Boss
First Cowboy
Second Cowboy
Third Cowboy
Cooky
Mayor of Deadwood
Bat Masterson

SETTING:
Tennessee, 1854–1869
Wild West, 1869–1890

© Macmillan/McGraw-Hill

First Narrator: Back in the days of the Wild West, there was one cowboy who could outride, outrope, and outshoot all the rest. He was an African American whose name was Nat Love, but everyone called him by his nickname, Deadwood Dick.

Second Narrator: Nat spent most of his life on the range—gentling wild horses, branding cattle, and herding steers across hundreds of miles of open prairie. Near the end of his life, Nat recorded all his adventures in an autobiography titled *The Life and Adventures of Nat Love, Better Known in the Cattle Country as "Deadwood Dick."* Many of the exciting adventures in its pages read like tall tales right out of the Wild West.

Nat: I was born a slave in an old log cabin in Tennessee in 1854. I never knew the exact day of my birth because in those days, no one thought to keep track of slave babies' birthdays. My pa worked on a plantation owned by a white man named Robert Love, and my ma was in charge of the kitchen in the big house.

First Narrator: When Nat turned eleven, his life suddenly changed. The Civil War was over, and Nat was now free. But freedom didn't make Nat's life much easier. His father died, and the Love family was poor and hungry. Nat knew that his family's survival depended on him.

Nat: There's no food left in the cupboard, Ma, and all the money you and Pa managed to save is gone. Someone has got to feed us, and I reckon that means me.

Mrs. Love: How will we ever get along without your pa? You're too young and too small to go out and work like a man.

Nat: I may be young, but I'm free. I'll use my freedom to go out and get a job. I was talking with Mr. Brooks today. He promised he would give me a job working on his farm. He's offering to pay me $1.50 a month—that's not a fortune, but something is better than nothing. I'm starting work tomorrow.

Mrs. Love: Your pa would be proud of you. Someday, you're going to grow up and make something of yourself. I just know it.

Nat: That's exactly what I aim to do, Ma.

Second Narrator: The very next day, Nat started his job and soon began bringing home potatoes, bacon, cornmeal, and molasses. He worked hard six days out of seven, and he always shared what he made with his mother and the other children in the family.

First Narrator: Then one Sunday—his day off—he found another job. This job was the start of his life as a cowboy. It all happened at a nearby horse ranch owned by Mr. Williams.

Mr. Williams: Hey, Nat! Come on over here. I want to talk with you for a minute.

Nat: Sure thing, Mr. Williams.

Mr. Williams: Looky here, Nat. I've got a bunch of wild horses that need gentling. Word has it that you're good with horses. Folks also say that there's not much that scares you.

Nat: Well, sir, horses don't scare me—wild or tamed. And I wouldn't mind making a little extra money.

Mr. Williams: Tell you what. I'll give you ten cents for every wild horse you can gentle for me. How does that sound?

Nat: That sounds just fine to me. You've got yourself a deal! Just lead me to the horse.

Second Narrator: Nat mounted one of Mr. Williams's wild horses and stuck to it like a leech. No matter how much the horse kicked and bucked, Nat clung to its back. Mr. Williams and Nat were both happy with the deal they had made. From then on, Nat spent Sundays breaking in horses and earning ten cents for each horse he gentled.

First Narrator: Then, one day, Mr. Williams talked to Nat about the wildest horse in his stable—a horse named Black Highwayman. Nobody had ever been able to stay on Black Highwayman's back long enough to ride him.

Mr. Williams: You've gentled a lot of horses for me in the past few months. But I've got one that's meaner and smarter than all the rest of 'em put together. For some reason, he just won't take to the feeling of a human on his back. Do you think you're ready to try to gentle Black Highwayman?

Nat: Sir, that horse has one mighty mean temper, and you and I both know it. I might be willing to try to gentle him, but I'm not willing to do it for ten cents.

Mr. Williams: Well, just what amount of money do you have in mind?

Nat: I was thinking about fifty cents. You know, I'm taking quite a risk getting on a mean horse like that.

Mr. Williams: It's a risk, all right, but fifty cents is too much. Would you be willing to do it for fifteen?

Nat: I value my life too much to throw it away for fifteen cents, Mr. Williams. How about twenty-five cents paid in advance?

Mr. Williams: It's a deal. Here's your money, and good luck.

Young Girl: Hey, Nat! Don't try to ride that horse. You'll get yourself killed for sure!

Nat: It's too late now! I just took the money, and I'm going to gentle that horse if it's the last thing I do. Just stand back and watch me.

Young Girl: Will you look at that! He's doing it. Nat's climbing up on Black Highwayman's back!

First Narrator: The second that Nat got on its back, Black Highwayman took off like a shot across the countryside. Nat knew he would either break the horse or break his neck.

Young Girl: Hang on, Nat!

First Narrator: He hung on for dear life until, finally, the horse wore itself out. With a big grin on his face, Nat brought the horse back to Mr. Williams's stable.

Young Girl: Hooray! You did it! You really earned that twenty-five cents.

First Narrator: But when Nat reached into his pocket to find his hard-earned money, it was gone. He had lost it on his wild ride!

Second Narrator: Nat remained home with his family until he turned fifteen. About that time, he got the urge to go out and see the world. He felt confident that he could take care of himself, so he said good-bye to his mother and headed out West. His

destination was Dodge City, Kansas. Located at the end of the Western Cattle Trail, Dodge City had the reputation of being one of the roughest and toughest towns on the frontier. There Nat met up with the trail boss and several cowboys from a big cattle spread in Texas.

Trail Boss: So, tenderfoot, I can tell you're new to these parts. Where are you from?

Nat: I was born and raised in the state of Tennessee, but ever since I can remember, I've always wanted to come out West to be a cowboy. It sounds like the kind of life for me.

First Cowboy: Tennessee, you say? Then you don't know a doggone thing about cattle raising or wild horses.

Nat: Is that so? Well, sir, I'll have you know that I've ridden a few wild horses in my time.

Second Cowboy: Why sure, son. You've ridden Tennessee horses— not real horses like we have out here. Horses in the West are different—they're wilder and meaner, just like us cowpokes.

Nat: That may be so, but I've never met a horse I couldn't ride.

Trail Boss: I'll tell you what, Nat. I've got a horse called Old Good Eye over in that corral. Now if you stick on that horse, you've got yourself a guaranteed job as a trail hand with my outfit. Is it a deal?

Nat: You bet it's a deal. Here's my handshake on it. I'll saddle up that pony right now and take him for a little ride.

Third Cowboy: This should be fun to watch. That tenderfoot doesn't know what he's in for.

First Cowboy: He thinks he can be a cowboy just by coming out West. Old Good Eye will teach Nat Love a lesson that he won't soon forget!

First Narrator: But before Nat got on the horse, another black cowboy by the name of Bronco Jim came over and gave Nat a few pointers about riding Old Good Eye. Nat thanked him kindly and then swung one leg over the horse's back. Old Good Eye started to buck like he was being stung by a swarm of hornets.

Trail Boss: By golly! Look at that horse go!

First Cowboy: Young Nat is bouncing mighty high in that saddle!

Second Cowboy: He's bouncing, all right, but he's staying on.

Second Narrator: Nat stuck on until that horse grew too tired to buck anymore. But later, he admitted that it was the worst ride of his entire life.

Nat: That horse rattled every bone in my body and then some!

Trail Boss: You did all right, Nat. And you earned yourself a place in this outfit.

First Narrator: The trail boss offered Nat a job that paid thirty dollars a month, and Nat took him up on his offer immediately. He left Dodge City with the outfit and rode with them to their ranch in the panhandle section of Texas.

Second Narrator: Before long, Nat became one of the best cowhands in the West. He loved the wild and free life on the range. He was good at roping and riding, and soon he became an expert at recognizing the hundreds of different brands used by the ranches to identify their livestock.

Trail Boss: Nat, I hear from the rest of the boys that you've got a good eye for reading brands.

Nat: Shucks, it's not that hard. Why, I can spot a "Double L" or a "Lazy Z" mark from a mile away.

Trail Boss: Well, I'd like to put you in charge of reading brands for this outfit. It will mean more work, but it will also mean a raise in pay.

First Narrator: So Nat worked with cowboys from other ranches during the roundups. Cattle from various ranches grazed together on the range, but a few times each year, they would be herded to a central place. There, cowhands from the different ranches would work together to sort them by brand, mark any new calves that had not yet been branded, and count to see how many head of cattle each ranch had.

Second Narrator: Without this kind of cooperation, the job would never have gotten done. Nat soon became well known among the cowboys for his fair play, and his skill at reading brands was recognized by everyone.

Nat: Now that the cattle are all branded, when is the next big cattle drive?

Trail Boss: Next week we have to drive nearly a thousand head of cattle over the Chisholm Trail. You'll have to be in the saddle pretty much night and day.

First Narrator: During the big cattle drives, cowboys rode hundreds of miles. They herded the cattle, leading them across rivers, protecting them, and otherwise making sure they arrived at the end of the trail unharmed. It was exhausting work.

Second Narrator: After a long day in the saddle, the cowboys gathered around the campfire to share a meal and trade a few stories.

Nat: This is good grub, Cooky. It's just what I need after fifteen hours in the saddle.

Cooky: I put extra hot pepper in it just for you. I know you like your stew hot and spicy!

Nat: Muchas gracias. All that chili pepper helps keep me warm inside on these cold nights.

Cooky: Speaking of cold nights, my blanket got soaked when we forded the river this afternoon.

Nat: Here, friend, take mine. I've got your hot pepper stew to keep me warm.

Cooky: Why, thanks. I heard tell you were a real compadre. Now I know it's the truth.

First Cowboy: Say, Nat, I heard a story about you last spring. Some cowpunchers up north Wyoming way were talking about how you saved a buddy of theirs during a blizzard.

Nat: Aw, any other cowboy would have done the same. You see, my buddy and I were stuck in this big snowstorm without horses, and he got hurt. I just carried him a bit till we met up with help. If we cowboys don't stick together, none of us will survive.

First Narrator: Being a cowboy was a rough life, all right. But nobody was better suited to it than Nat Love. He was good at riding and roping and shooting. But, best of all, he could think straight in a tight situation and find a way out of it.

Second Narrator: Nat's thinking ability came in real handy one night on the prairie in the Nebraska Territory. Nat was standing watch with a couple of other cowboys after a long day on the trail.

Nat: Look up at that big old moon. It sure puts me in mind of singing a song.

Second Cowboy: Maybe you had better not. You might scare the cattle. And we just got 'em all settled down for the night.

Nat: I guess you're right. My singing never was appreciated by man or beast.

Third Cowboy: Why don't we all just turn in early? The sky is as clear as can be. There's no chance of a storm spooking the herd. And there are too many of us for cattle rustlers to mess with. What do you say, Nat?

Nat: Sorry, partner, I hate to disagree, but I say we keep watch. You never know what might happen out here on the prairie. We've got over a thousand head of cattle in this herd, and if anything happened to them, I sure wouldn't want to be caught napping by the trail boss.

First Cowboy: Nat's right, but it surely is a peaceful night. How could anything go wrong on a night like this? Well, boys, I'll take the first watch.

First Narrator: An hour later, Nat suddenly jumped up out of his bedroll and looked to the north.

Nat: What's that noise in the distance? It sounds a lot like thunder.

First Cowboy: I don't hear a thing. It's only your imagination. Just look at that sky—there's no storm brewing tonight.

Third Cowboy: No, Nat's right. There is a roaring sound coming from up north. But it's too loud and too steady to be thunder.

Nat: It's buffalo, boys! There's a buffalo stampede heading right for us! We've got to get the cattle out of their way. Rouse all the hands and tell them to saddle up, pronto! We've got to try to drive the cattle out of the path of those buffalo!

Second Cowboy: Boys, this sure is going to be some night!

First Narrator: It was some night, all right. Nat and the rest of the cowboys did all they could to move the cattle out of the way. They even rode straight into the buffalo stampede, trying to turn the animals aside. After hours of riding and herding and yelling, it was all over.

Trail Boss: Now that the dust has settled, Nat, can you give me some idea of just how bad things are?

Nat: Well, sir, we lost only five head of cattle, but something worse happened. Cal Surcey—that young cowhand who just hired on—got thrown from his horse and was trampled to death by the buffalo.

Second Narrator: Nat and the other cowhands buried Cal and then, with heavy hearts, they herded the cattle on up the trail to Wyoming.

First Narrator: A few years later, in 1876, Nat's outfit got an order to deliver three thousand head of cattle to Deadwood City in the Dakota Territory. It was a long ride, and by the time the cowboys arrived in Deadwood, they were ready to celebrate.

Second Narrator: Now it just so happened that the next day was Independence Day. And on that day, the town of

Deadwood planned to hold a big roping contest for all the cowboys who were in the area. Since it was a holiday, cowpunchers from all over the territory rode into Deadwood City for the competition.

Trail Boss: Hey there, Nat! We're counting on you to enter that roping contest and win it. You're the best cowhand in our outfit. In all my years of cow-punching, I've never seen anybody handle a rope or a horse like you do.

Nat: You'd have to tie me up to keep me out of that contest, boss. I hear they've rounded up the wildest broncos in the territory for us to ride.

Trail Boss: You heard right about that, Nat. But there isn't a horse alive that you can't stick to once you've made up your mind to it.

First Narrator: Nat entered the contest, but so did a lot of other cowboys. Each of them had to choose a wild bronco to rope and ride. The cowboy who finished the contest in the fastest time would be the winner. Well, in nine minutes flat, Nat roped, threw, tied, bridled, saddled, and mounted his bronco. Then he rode it until that horse was as tame as a kitten. No other cowboy came even close to his time. The crowd went wild with excitement.

Mayor: Nat Love, the fair town of Deadwood would like to make you an honorary citizen. You've earned yourself the title of Deadwood Dick, Champion Roper of the West.

Nat: I'm pleased and flattered that you'd give me a nickname in honor of this fine town. Deadwood Dick—that's a handle any cowhand would be proud to carry.

Third Cowboy: The day's not over yet, Nat . . . er, I mean, Deadwood Dick. The shooting contest is coming up next. Are you going to win that one, too?

Nat: I aim to give it my best shot. But there's some mighty mean competition ahead. I see my old pal Stormy Jim over there by the corral, and if I'm not mistaken, that's Powder Horn Bill near the hitching post. I hear they never miss anything they aim at.

Mayor: Come on, Deadwood Dick. Show us how well you can shoot!

Second Narrator: Well, Nat Love proved that he was the best all-around cowboy in the Dakota Territory. He won both the rifle- and the Colt 45-shooting contests!

Mayor: Well, I suppose this makes you the official hero of Deadwood City. It is my pleasure to award you the $200 prize money.

Nat: Thank you kindly, Mayor.

Second Narrator: From that day on, Nat Love was known through-out cattle country as Deadwood Dick.

First Narrator: For fourteen more years, Nat rode the range as a cowboy. His life was filled with one adventure after another. Once he was captured by Indians. They respected the way he had fought, so they nursed his wounds and adopted him into the tribe. After some weeks, though, Nat made a daring escape, riding bareback for a hundred miles to his home in Texas. Another time, Nat almost froze to death during a prairie blizzard, but his luck and his courage pulled him through.

Second Narrator: By 1890, the old Wild West was fading out of existence and becoming another chapter in the

history of America. Nat talked about its passing with his old friend Bat Masterson, the famous sheriff of Dodge City.

Nat: It's real sad what's happening to the West. The buffalo are almost all gone. Houses are being built right smack dab in the middle of the trail where we used to drive herds of cattle up to Dodge City.

Bat Masterson: And I hear that the ranches are all fenced in with that newfangled barbed wire, and almost all the cattle are shipped by rail nowadays.

Nat: I surely don't know what the West is coming to, but one thing is certain—they don't need old cowboys like me anymore.

Bat Masterson: What are you going to do with yourself if your range-riding days are over?

Nat: I'll tell you one thing I'm not going to do. I plumb refuse to sit around here and mope and grow old. I'm thinking about heading over to Denver, Colorado, and hunting down a job there. If the country is going to change, then I'm going to change with it!

Bat Masterson: You always were a fighter. Best of luck to you in Denver.

First Narrator: Nat moved to Denver, leaving his cowboy life behind him forever. There, he met the woman who was to become Mrs. Nat Love. They got married and settled down in Denver. A short while later, Nat took a job as a Pullman porter on the Denver and Rio Grande Railroad. Soon, he was rolling across the range behind an iron horse instead of riding across it on the back of a real one.

Second Narrator: As the years passed, Nat often thought back on his days as a cowboy. He decided to write down all the exciting adventures that had come his way as the famous cowboy, Deadwood Dick. Nat summed up what it was like to be a cowboy with these words:

Nat: I, Nat Love, now in my fifty-fourth year, hale, hearty, and happy, will ever cherish a fond and loving feeling for the old days on the range, its exciting adventures, good horses, good and bad men, long venturesome rides, and—last but foremost—the friends I have made and the friends I have gained.

First Narrator: And so ends the story of Nat Love, better known in cattle country as Deadwood Dick.

ALL THE MONEY IN THE WORLD

based on the novel by Bill Brittain

by Richard Holland

CAST:

Narrator
Vincent Arbor
Roselynn Peabody
Quentin Stowe
Flan
Mr. Stowe
Mrs. Stowe
President

General Mainwaring
Sergeant
Mr. Milleridge
Mrs. Hobson
Miss Draymore
Mayor
Mrs. Trussker

SETTING:

A small farming community

Narrator: On a lazy summer day, in a town not too far away, three friends sat on a river bank fishing and wishing—just wishing and fishing.

Vincent: You know what I wish? I wish I could be a policeman like my dad, right now, without waiting to grow up.

Roselynn: I wish I'd win a gold medal in the Olympics someday. But right now I'd really like to have my own color TV and . . . oh, lots of things. What about you, Quentin?

Quentin: Well, coming over here today, I was wishing I owned a new ten-speed bike. My old bike is really rickety.

Roselynn: I'm glad my dad can't hear us talking this way. He says I spend too much time wishing for things.

Vincent: That sounds just like my father. He says I do too much daydreaming and not enough homework. Do you get into trouble for daydreaming, Quentin?

Quentin: Yeah. At breakfast I wished I had ten dollars to spend any way I wanted. But when Poppa heard me, he said, "Stop all this foolishness. I don't want to hear any more talk about money."

Roselynn: Hey! Maybe that's why the three of us get along so well. Each of us can wish for whatever we want and know the other two won't laugh when we talk about it.

Quentin: Well, right now I just wish I could catch a really big fish so I could take it home for supper. Wait! I've got a bite! It's a big one!

Roselynn: Be careful, Quent! Don't pull too hard or you'll break the line!

Quentin: Okay . . . I'll be . . . careful.

Vincent: Wow! Did you see that fish jump? It's huge!

Quentin: Help . . . me . . . pull it in!

Roselynn: Okay! We've got hold of you! Ready? One . . . two . . . three. . . . Pull!

Quentin: We did it! Wow! It's the biggest bass I've ever seen! I'd better take it right home. See you later.

Roselynn: When?

Quentin: Let's all meet at my house this afternoon. I'll have my chores done by then.

Vincent: Okay. So long.

Narrator: Quentin's wish to catch a big fish had come true. So as he pedaled home on his old, rusty bicycle, he wished for bigger things.

Quentin: I wish I had a ten-speed bike like Roselynn's . . . and a new coat for Momma . . . and a tractor that really ran right for Poppa. And maybe even . . .

Narrator: Just then there was a loud POP! Then a long psssss.

Quentin: Oh, no! Not another flat tire! By the time I get it fixed, this fish will spoil in the sun. Wait a minute, there's a well. Good! I'll put my fish in the bucket and drop the bucket into the water. That should keep it fresh.

Flan: Hey, you up there! Don't drop that bucket on my head!

Quentin: Is somebody down there?

Flan: I am! Now, are you going to help a poor old man or not?

Quentin: How far down are you?

Flan: Since I'm standing up to my knees in water, I'd say I was on the bottom. Have you a rope or something?

Quentin: All I have is a fishing pole.

Flan: Splendid. Just lower it down to me.

Quentin: The line is not very strong.

Flan: You'd be surprised how little I weigh, lad. Just lower it down, and we'll make do.

Quentin: All right. Here it comes.

Flan: I see it. . . . Just a bit farther. . . . Ah, I've got it. Haul away, lad!

Quentin: You are very light. Are you okay?

Flan: You're doing fine. Another couple of feet and I'll be out.

Narrator: Quentin pulled up on his fishing pole until a hand grasped the side of the well. It was a tiny hand, no bigger than the hand of a doll. But, more amazing than the size was the color—it was green.

Flan: That's it, lad, I'm out. The wet and the dark are more than a body should have to bear.

Narrator: Quentin was wide-eyed with wonder. It was a man, but one such as Quentin had never seen before. He was no bigger than a doll. His face, like his hands, was pale green and wrinkled with age. On his head, which was no bigger than a baseball, sat a tiny top hat. And in his teeth, he held the stem of a tiny pipe.

Quentin: Hello . . . sir. I'm Quentin Stowe. And you'd be . . .?

Flan: I'd best be on my way, thanking you very much for pulling me out of the well.

Quentin: Hey, wait! I saved your life. The least you can do is tell me who you are.

Narrator: Quentin's fishing pole gave a jerk—the silver hook was snagged in the man's coattails.

Flan: I wonder if you'd be so kind as to take the hook out of my coattails, lad. It's hard to reach back there.

Quentin: I will, but first tell me who you are.

Flan: No good will come of this, lad. But since you must know, I'm called Flan.

Quentin: Flan. That's an unusual name. What kind of a person are you, Mr. Flan?

Flan: Not mister. Just plain Flan. I'm what folks call a leprechaun. I come from Ireland. Just what is it you're staring at?

Quentin: I never saw anybody with green skin before.

Flan: Now don't go making fun of me because of my color. Green's just as good as black or white or purple or gold or whatever color skin comes in these days. Besides, what's another color between friends?

Quentin: You may be in for trouble. Poppa says that sometimes people with different skin colors don't get along too well together.

Flan: The first person who tries something with me because of my color, I'll give him green skin, I will. I'll turn him into a frog.

Quentin: You can do that?

© Macmillan/McGraw-Hill

Flan: If you know anything at all about leprechauns, you know we can do all sorts of magic.

Quentin: If you can do magic, why couldn't you get out of the well? Why did you need my help?

Flan: Because I fell asleep in school during the lesson on flying. The lesson was terribly complicated, and the day was hot, and I was tired. I dozed off, and the result is that I can't fly. There was no way out of the well until you came along. Now, lad, you must claim your due.

Quentin: My due?

Flan: You caught me fair and square, and you made me say my name. By the Law of the Leprechauns, I must grant you three wishes.

Quentin: Three wishes! Wow! Can I wish for anything?

Flan: Anything at all. But I'd best warn you. Whatever you wish for, that's what you'll get. And you'll have it for all time.

Quentin: I guess I'd better think about this. But right now I'd better be getting home. Would you like to come along?

Flan: Don't mind if I do. I was living in a cozy nook under a nice porch that belonged to a Mrs. Viola Trussker. But her singing got to be too much for me—such whooping and shrieking! I had to leave. Where do you live?

Quentin: Four miles from here. I wish my bike was fixed. Then we'd be home in no time.

Narrator: There was a rumble of thunder and the very air seemed to vibrate. Then suddenly, the bike's flat tire was filled with air.

Flan: First wish granted. Hop aboard.

Quentin: That's not fair! That wasn't a real wish.

Flan: I'm afraid it was, lad.

Quentin: I wish there was a way to keep from making wishes that I don't want to make.

Flan: Easy as pie. We won't consider your third wish fully made until you count to three after you've made it.

Quentin: My third wish? What do you mean? What happened to the second one?

Flan: You just had it, wishing not to make wishes you don't wish to wish. You have one wish left.

Quentin: But I. . . . Oh my, this wish business is more complicated than I thought it would be.

Flan: Give your last one careful thought. And don't forget to count to three afterward.

Narrator: There were so many things Quentin wanted. The new bike, the things for Momma and Poppa, money for . . . money! That was it!

Quentin: I know! I wish . . . I wish for all the money in the world. One . . . two . . . THREE!

Narrator: For a moment there was only silence. Then there was a tremendous WHUMPH, followed by noises as if the sky were tearing apart. Finally, there was an eerie quiet.

Flan: Open your eyes, Quentin. Your wish has been granted.

Narrator: Slowly Quentin opened his eyes. He saw fields and cows and birds, but no money.

Quentin: It was all just talk, wasn't it, Flan?

Flan: I wouldn't trick you, lad. You wanted all the money in the world, and you've got it. But it's more than anyone can carry.

Narrator: Disappointed, Quentin pedaled his bike slowly toward the farm. But when the house came into view, he could barely see it. There were huge mounds of something where his father's crops used to be. It was . . .

Quentin: All the money in the world!

Narrator: Yes, piles of money that almost touched the clouds! Quentin ran to the nearest pile and plunged his arms in up to his shoulders. He picked up wads of bills and tossed them into the air. There were dollars and Mexican pesos and English pounds and Indian rupees and Dutch guilders and German marks—so many different kinds of money.

Quentin: Money! Money! Money, money, money, moneeeeeeeeeeey!

Narrator: Quentin tramped on mounds of gold and silver coins. Finally, he came to the fence at the edge of the road, where Flan was seated on the top rail. The little leprechaun was wearing a wide grin on his face.

Flan: See, lad? I kept my promise, didn't I? Who's this now?

Mr. Stowe: Quentin? What's going on here? What's all this stuff where the crops used to be?

Quentin: We've got something better than crops, Poppa. We've got all the money in the world!

Mr. Stowe: And I suppose Cinderella is coming to dinner tonight. Quentin, when you start with this daydreaming business, I just don't want to listen.

Quentin: But it's true, Poppa. It really is!

Mr. Stowe: All this paper can't be worth a hill of beans.

Flan: It's worth what all the money in the world is worth to anyone who has it.

Mr. Stowe: Who's that little green man?

Narrator: As Quentin and Flan told Mr. Stowe the story of what happened, Vincent and Roselynn arrived on their bicycles. They listened in silence. Then Vincent gave out a yell.

Vincent: Wow! Oh, wow! Think of all the things you can buy!

Quentin: Think of all the things we can buy! Here, take all you want. You, too, Roselynn.

Narrator: Roselynn and Vincent grabbed handfuls of money and stuffed the bills into their pockets and into their shirts and socks and shoes. When they were through, they looked round, fat, and lumpy.

Roselynn: Oh, Quentin! Gee, thanks! This is wonderful.

Narrator: Vincent and Roselynn waddled out onto the road. As they did, PONG! PONG! They weren't fat or round or lumpy any more. All the money they had stuffed into their clothing sat in two neat piles on the side of the road.

Vincent: My money! It's gone! All of it's gone!

Roselynn: So's mine! I bet Quentin told Flan to take it all back!

Quentin: Now wait a minute. I didn't!

Vincent: You never really meant for us to have any of the money, did you, Quentin?

Roselynn: Come on, Vincent. Let's go. We can still have fun, just the two of us.

Narrator: Quentin was very unhappy. His best friends were mad at him, and his poppa was upset and worried. This money business wasn't going the way he had planned. Flan, Mr. Stowe, and Quentin went in the house to see Mrs. Stowe. They had to figure out what to do about all that money.

Mrs. Stowe: What are all those piles where the crops used to be? And who is this little green man? Isn't he the cutest thing!

Quentin: It's all the money in the world, Momma.

Mrs. Stowe: All the money in the world? It can't possibly be!

Quentin: It is, Momma. And this is Flan. He's a leprechaun, and he gave me the money.

Mrs. Stowe: But where did it come from? And what are you going to do with it?

Mr. Stowe: Those are very good questions. I have a feeling we'll find the answers on the news. Quentin, turn on the TV.

Quentin: Yes, Poppa. Wow! The President's on! He's making a speech.

President: Fellow citizens, today something happened that has never before occurred in our history—the whole money supply of Washington, D.C., has disappeared. We have reports of money missing from Fort Knox and other locations, as well.

We don't know how this happened. Until we find the money, most government work will have to stop. The situation is serious—quite serious—but not hopeless. In the meantime, we are planning to negotiate some loans from our allies abroad.

Mrs. Stowe: Quentin, how much money did you say was out there?

Quentin: All the money in the world.

President: I have appointed General Linus Mainwaring to locate the missing money. General, do you have anything to say?

General: Yes, sir, Mr. President. I just want to say this to whoever has that money: We're going to find you, mister. And when we do—watch out!

Narrator: For the next two days Quentin saw how his wish affected the entire town. No one had money to buy anything. Stores were closing. Food was spoiling on the shelves. People were very upset. Quentin sat on top of a pile of money wondering what to do. Flan just relaxed on Quentin's shoulder. Suddenly, there was a low rumble. Then off in the distance . . .

Quentin: Trucks! Lots of them, coming this way! Look on the sides of the trucks—it says United States Army!

Narrator: The trucks screeched to a halt and a uniformed man jumped out. He had row after row of medals on his chest. Quentin recognized him from TV. It was General Mainwaring! He was followed by his staff sergeant.

General: It's the money, all right, just where our observation planes spotted it. Sergeant, tell the

troops to advance across the fence and surround the money.

Sergeant: Advance across the fence and surround the money!

General: You! You with that green thing on your shoulder. What's your name? And how did all this money get here?

Quentin: My name is Quentin Stowe, sir. And this is Flan. He brought the money here.

General: I see. Well, I'm here on orders from the President of the United States. We will now proceed to load up the money. Sergeant! Load the trucks. Take the gold bars first.

Sergeant: Load up the money! Take the gold bars first!

Narrator: The soldiers loaded three trucks full of gold bars. It took them half the day, gold being as heavy as it is. The trucks sagged under the weight of the bars.

General: Move the trucks out!

Sergeant: Move the trucks out!

Narrator: The trucks pulled off the grass onto the road. PONG! PONG! PONG! The rear of each truck bounced up into the air, but when it came back down, the truck was no longer sagging.

Sergeant: General, the gold . . . it's not in the trucks any more. It's gone!

Quentin: It's not gone, sir. It's over here in the field.

General: You mean the gold went back onto the farm?

Quentin: Yes, sir. The money keeps coming back.

General: Impossible! Sergeant, have the troops surround the farm! Nobody touches this money! Set up tents and make camp. We may be here a while.

Narrator: Quentin's troubles went from bad to worse. Not only were all the people in town suffering because of his wish, but the United States Army was now living on his family's farm. He had to do something, but what?

Quentin: I know! I'll go shopping and spend some of my money. That way the store owners can keep their stores open.

Narrator: Quentin stuffed his pockets full of coins and twenty dollar bills. To his delight, the money stayed in his pockets when he left the farm. He headed toward town with Flan. His first stop was at Mr. Milleridge's Ice Cream Store.

Mr. Milleridge: Oh, it's you, Quentin. Maybe you haven't heard, but I'm quitting the ice cream business. And it's all your fault! By the way, who's he?

Quentin: His name is Flan.

Mr. Milleridge: He's green, ain't he?

Quentin: Yes. He's three hundred years old.

Mr. Milleridge: I guess anyone would turn green after three hundred years.

Quentin: May we have ice cream sodas, please? I have the money.

Mr. Milleridge: Money? You've got real money? Well, why didn't you say so? You can have anything you want—if you've got the money to pay for it.

Narrator: When Quentin and Flan finished their sodas, Quentin paid for them with four quarters.

They then made their way to Hobson's Clothing Store.

Mrs. Hobson: Good day, Quentin. I didn't think you'd take the time off from counting all your money to come visiting.

Quentin: I'm here to buy Momma a nice warm coat for when it turns cold. I have the money.

Mrs. Hobson: You have money? If you have money, we have coats!

Narrator: Mrs. Hobson took Quentin right to the best coats. She helped him pick out a coat that was thick and warm. Quentin gave her six twenty-dollar bills. Next stop was the jewelry store!

Quentin: Miss Draymore, I want a real nice watch for my father. I have the money right here.

Miss Draymore: Would you like a gold watch or a silver watch? Or maybe you would like one with jewels!

Mrs. Hobson: Stop! Don't sell him a thing! Quentin, you tricked us! The money you gave me has vanished!

Mr. Milleridge: Hold everything! Where is it? My money—where is it? You bought two sodas in my store. You paid for them with four quarters. No sooner were you out the door than the money was gone!

Quentin: Oh, no! The money's back in my pocket!

Flan: The money's yours for all time. You can take it anywhere you'd like. But if you give it to someone else, you won't have all the money in the world anymore. So it has to return to you.

Miss Draymore: No watch for you, young man!

Mrs. Hobson: And I will take back that coat, thank you very much!

Mr. Milleridge: Quentin, you and your green friend—follow me!

Narrator: Mr. Milleridge couldn't take his ice cream sodas back, so he made Quentin and Flan clean his basement. But Flan didn't think the mishap was his fault, so Quentin had to do all the cleaning himself.

Quentin: What good is having all the money in the world? I'm working twice as hard as I did when I had none!

Narrator: Quentin's idea to solve the money shortage didn't work out. So that evening, the mayor called a town meeting that everyone was required to attend.

Mayor: As mayor of this town, I have a plan to solve the money problem. Here are four boxes of play money I found in Mr. Reese's Variety Store. The money is called "dillies." We will use dillies as money until we figure out a way to get the real money off the Stowe farm.

Mr. Milleridge: That sounds like a fine idea.

Mrs. Hobson: Yes, I think it will do nicely.

Mayor: Now, everyone who earns money get into line. Each of you will come up and tell me how much you earn in a week. Then I'll give you that much in dillies.

Narrator: The mayor handed out dilly bills until everyone in town was satisfied.

Mayor: If anyone has any debts to pay off, this would be a good time to do it.

Narrator: There was a rustling of bills as people exchanged dilly money.

Mayor: Now we're all settled up, and the town can get back to normal.

Narrator: That's what he thought. PONG! All the dillies appeared in Quentin's lap!

Quentin: Not again!

Mr. Milleridge: Quentin's got my dillies!

Mrs. Hobson: Mine, too!

Flan: You fools, don't you see what has happened? You turned dillies into real money when you used them to pay off debts. Now that dillies are real money, they are part of all the money in the world. So Quentin gets them.

Mr. Milleridge: I want my dillies back!

Narrator: Just then, General Mainwaring stormed into the town meeting.

General: Attention! Quentin Stowe! You're coming with me. You have an appointment to keep—an appointment with the President of the United States.

Narrator: Quentin and Flan were rushed off to Washington, D.C., by helicopter. The President was waiting for them on the steps of the White House.

President: Hello, Quentin. Let's go to the Oval Office. It's the right place to discuss big problems, and today we have a very big problem on our hands. Quentin, why don't you just tell me how you came to have all that money.

Narrator: As they walked to the Oval Office, Quentin explained how it all started with his wishing for a ten-speed bicycle. Then he told about meeting Flan and his wish for all the money in the world and how it came true.

President: And now you can't wish the money away because you have no wishes left?

Quentin: That's right, Mr. President. And I can't even spend the money. It's been nothing but a big problem ever since I got it.

President: The problem is even bigger than you think. All the people of the world need things to live—things that take money to buy. But you have all the money.

Quentin: I'd give it all back if I could.

President: I believe you would. But some countries think the United States is keeping the money on purpose. And because of that, they are threatening to declare war.

Quentin: War! They can't do that!

President: I'm afraid they not only can, Quentin, but they will. Flan, is there any way you can make the money go back to where it belongs?

Flan: No, sir. He caught me and made me say my name. That's the only way a leprechaun grants wishes. Except . . . I'll say no more!

President: So there is a way for Quentin to get more wishes, isn't there, Flan? What is it? You must tell us!

Flan: I can't tell you. The Law of the Leprechauns won't allow me to say. My punishment will be fearful if

I do. You must live by your laws, and I must live by mine.

President: Well, Quentin, if there is an answer, you'll have to find it. The whole country—indeed, the whole world—is depending on you.

Narrator: Back home, the mayor called another town meeting. Everyone was there, and they were more angry than ever. And they were most angry at Flan!

Mr. Milleridge: It's his fault! Quentin could never have gotten the money without him! He's small, he's wrinkled, and he's GREEN! If he weren't green, we'd probably have our money!

Miss Draymore: Yes! It's horrible! He's green!

All: He's green! He's green! He's green! He's GREEN!

Narrator: Flan stood there with a big, green grin on his face. He tapped his toe three times and WHAMO! All were silent. They were frozen like statues.

Flan: Now I'll have my say. Quentin made a foolish wish, but today the rest of you are being even more foolish. Because of the way you talked to me, I'm leaving town forever. And with me goes any chance of the money ever being returned. I can't help being green, just as Quentin couldn't help making a boy's wish.

Narrator: Flan snapped his fingers as he rushed out the door. Everyone was freed from the spell, and they rushed to follow him. Suddenly, from outside, they heard a loud CR-R-R-UNCH! Flan had fallen through a rotted-out section of the Town Hall steps, and now he was stuck up to his waist!

Flan: Don't anyone come near me! I'll change you all into caterpillars! Oh, fie on the day I slept through that flying lesson. Woe is me!

Quentin: You're stuck, Flan. Do you want me to help you get out?

Flan: No, lad. I will not beg! So don't think I will.

Narrator: At that moment, Quentin was sure he knew Flan's secret.

Quentin: That's it! I can get three more wishes if you beg me to save you. Isn't that it, Flan?

Flan: Not three more wishes, just one. But don't think I'll beg you, lad. Especially after the way you made a mess of your last wish.

Quentin: Then I'll just have to ask Mrs. Trussker to sing for you.

Narrator: Mrs. Trussker was the worst singer in the world. People said she could sour milk just by singing near a cow.

Quentin: Mrs. Trussker, Flan likes your singing very much. Could you please oblige him with a song?

Mrs. Trussker: Why, Quentin, it would be my pleasure, [sings] Daisy, Daisy, give me your answer, do. I'm half crazy, All for the love of yewww. . . .

Flan: No, Quentin! It's cruel torture, that's what it is!

Mrs. Trussker: It won't be a stylish marriage, I can't afford a carriage, But you'll look sweet . . .

Flan: Enough! Make her stop!

Mrs. Trussker: Upon the seat of a bicycle built for twoooooooo!

Flan: I give up, Quentin! I beg you to save me, and I'll grant you one more wish!

Narrator: Quentin took Flan's hand and gently pulled him out of the hole in the steps.

Flan: Make your wish quickly, lad. Then I'm leaving this town as fast as my legs will carry me.

Narrator: Quentin closed his eyes.

Quentin: I wish . . . for all the money in the world to go back to where it belongs. One . . . two . . . THREE!

Narrator: Quentin opened his eyes. The first thing he saw was Flan scurrying down the street. Then he heard . . .

Mr. Milleridge: It's money! Real money! Sixteen dollars and thirty-two cents, right here in my pocket!

Mayor: The money's back in the bank! Piles and piles of it!

Narrator: Yes, the money was back in the banks and the houses and the pockets where it belonged. All the townspeople breathed a sigh of relief as they headed back to their homes and families. Happiest of all, Quentin went home and had his first good sleep in days. The next morning, he woke to the sight of the crops growing in the fields once again. As he finished up his chores, he looked up to find Vincent and Roselynn at the kitchen door, asking him to go fishing.

Vincent: I'm sorry I acted the way I did, Quentin. Money makes people do funny things.

Roselynn: I'm sorry, too, Quentin. Money isn't as important as friends. And the three of us are best friends.

Narrator: Just then there was the rumble of a truck coming up the road. It was an army truck, and when it stopped, General Mainwaring jumped out.

Quentin: Oh, no! Not again! What's happened now?

Narrator: The sergeant hopped out of the back, pulling something big. He was smiling.

General: Quentin Stowe!

Quentin: Yes, sir?

General: The President sent me to tell you that he isn't little and he isn't green and he can't grant your every wish. But there is one thing he can grant you—a new ten-speed bicycle! It's the best that money can buy.

Quentin: Thank you, sir! Vincent! Roselynn! Let's go for a spin!

Narrator: The general saluted as the three friends rode away with their fishing poles. They were off for a day of fishing—yes, fishing, but not too much wishing.

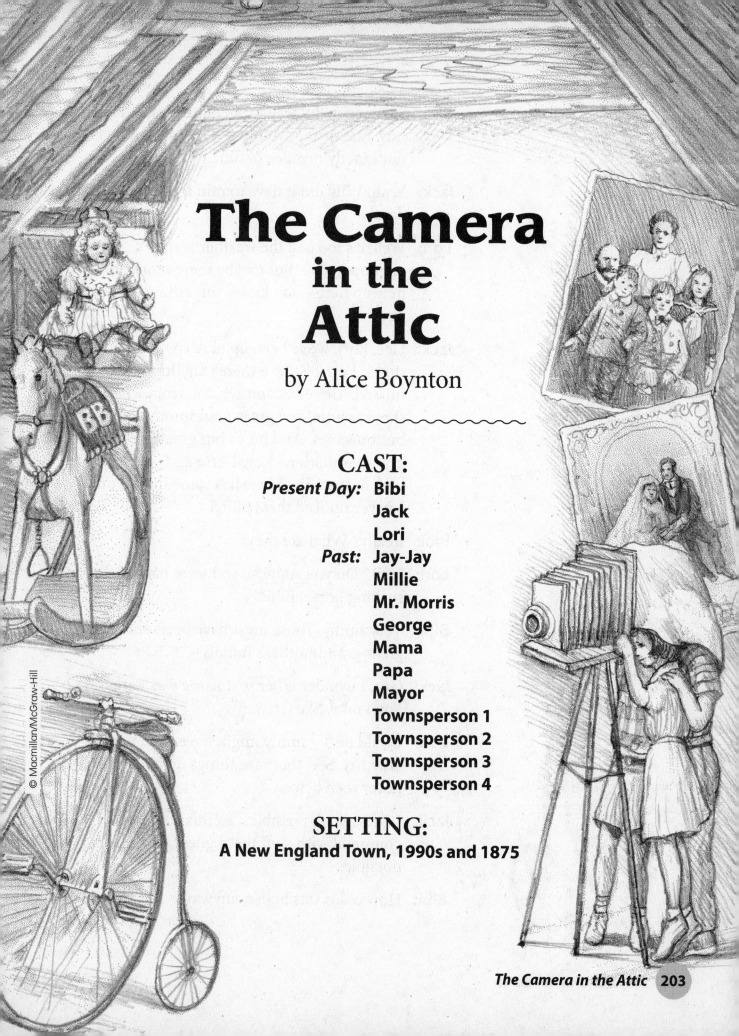

The Camera
in the
Attic

by Alice Boynton

CAST:

Present Day: Bibi
Jack
Lori

Past: Jay-Jay
Millie
Mr. Morris
George
Mama
Papa
Mayor
Townsperson 1
Townsperson 2
Townsperson 3
Townsperson 4

SETTING:
A New England Town, 1990s and 1875

© Macmillan/McGraw-Hill

Bibi: What an awful way to spend the Fourth of July. Just sitting around in Grammy's attic is not exactly my idea of fun.

Jack: Yeah. Why did it have to rain today of all days!

Lori: Well, it's too bad the weather is so uncooperative. But maybe there's something new up here—you know, something old that's new.

Jack: Gee, Lori, we've been up here so many times. I can't believe there's anything we've missed. There's Grammy's doll from when she was little, and great-grandmother's high-button shoes. And here's our great-great-grandmother's rocking horse and . . . Hey, look at that. The horse has some initials on it. I never noticed that before.

Bibi: Really? What are they?

Lori: "B.B." Do you suppose you were named after a rocking horse, Bibi?

Bibi: Very funny. Those must have been our great-great-grandmother's initials—"B.B."

Jack: Gee, I wonder if her first name was Barbara? You know, like Grammy.

Lori: Could be. Grammy might have been named after her. See, there are things up here we've never seen before.

Jack: I guess that's possible. . . . This attic is so crammed with stuff that I guess anything is possible.

Bibi: How old is this house, anyway?

© Macmillan/McGraw-Hill

Lori: Grammy says it's one of the oldest houses in Johnsbury. It's been here for five generations.

Bibi: Wouldn't that mean it was built when our great-great-grandparents were alive?

Jack: Wow! Talk about old.

Bibi: That would make it more than a hundred years old! Is that right?

Jack: I don't know. You're the math whiz, Bibi. If you say so, that's good enough for me. Hey, Lori, what are you doing now?

Lori: I'm checking out this thing in the corner. It's on some kind of old wooden tripod.

Jack: It looks like an old camera—a real old one. It's the kind where the photographer had to get under a hood to snap the picture.

Bibi: Hey, let's set it up. Maybe it still works.

Jack: That old thing? Impossible! Those cameras didn't even use film. They used special glass plates treated with chemicals that recorded the picture. And developing the photograph was really complicated. There's no way you could still use it.

Bibi: How come you know so much about photography all of a sudden?

Jack: Well, maybe one of our ancestors was a famous photographer—and it's in my genes. . . . Where did Lori disappear to now?

Lori: I'm here, under the hood of this camera. This is really weird. I don't get it.

Jack: What do you mean?

© Macmillan/McGraw-Hill

Lori: Come see for yourself.

Bibi: Move over, you two! Make room for me under there!

Lori: See what I mean? When you look through the viewfinder, you see something. But it's not the attic. It's a house!

Bibi: Yeah . . . and it looks kind of familiar, too. In fact, if the two trees in front weren't so small, and if there were hedges on the sides, I would say it was this house.

Jack: Hey, do you feel as if we're moving?

Bibi: Yes! We're going into the picture!

Lori: Whoaaa! Hang on!

Bibi: What happened? We're not in the attic any more. We're outside! What's going on here?

Lori: Look over there! It's Grammy's house.

Jack: No, it isn't. It's the house we saw in the camera. We're on the front lawn, and here's the camera from Grammy's attic!

Jay-Jay: That's right. So it is.

Lori: Who are you?

Jack: How did this guy get here? He looks like he's right out of the last century!

Bibi: Where are we? Where did you come from?

Jay-Jay: Hold on! My name is Jay-Jay, and I live here. I have been looking forward to a visit from you. Welcome at last!

Lori: Do you mean you were expecting us?

Jay-Jay: In a way. I've been waiting for you to look into the camera. There is a whole world for you to discover behind the lens.

Jack: What world?

Jay-Jay: Your whole history, you might say. And now you're here, right in the middle of it.

Millie: Oh, Jay-Jay—Mr. Morris the iceman is here. Mama has been waiting for him.

Lori: Wait a minute! Where did you come from?

Millie: Oh, just from across the street. I was over there petting Mr. Morris's horse. I like to give Elsie a lump of sugar whenever Mr. Morris comes by with the ice. She's a real nice horse. And Mr. Morris is real nice, too. Sometimes he even lets me help him drive the ice wagon.

Bibi: Lori! Jack! She's not kidding. There is a horse across the street—and a wagon loaded with blocks of ice, too.

Lori: I don't get any of this. Who are all these people?

Jack: And where are we?

Bibi: I don't know. It's strange, but it's kind of fun. Who's this?

Mr. Morris: Good morning, folks. Are you sure you have enough room for all this ice, Jay-Jay? Your ma asked me for a sixty-pound block.

Millie: We need the extra for ice cream, Mr. Morris. I'm going to help Mama make it. I volunteered to turn the crank on our brand new ice-cream freezer. We got it just in time for the celebration.

The Camera in the Attic 207

Bibi:	What celebration?
Mr. Morris:	Why, the Fourth of July celebration, of course!
Millie:	We're having a family picnic. That's why Jay-Jay is setting up his camera. He is going to take a picture of everyone in front of the house.
Jack:	I'm a good photographer, Jay-Jay. Maybe I can help you.
Jay-Jay:	That's the spirit, Jack. Now you're getting into it!
Jack:	But I still don't get it.
Jay-Jay:	You will!
Mr. Morris:	We had better get this ice into the icebox. It's starting to melt.
Lori:	What's an icebox?
Millie:	What's an icebox? Why, it's a tall wooden box with two sections in it. You put your food in the bottom section and your ice in the top one. The ice keeps the food cold. It even keeps milk from turning sour for two whole days. Don't you have an icebox?
Lori:	No, we have a refrigerator.
Millie:	What's a refrigerator?
Lori:	Well, it's a box that keeps food cold, too. Most refrigerators have a section that's so cold, you can make ice!
Mr. Morris:	Well, thank goodness we do not have refrigerators here! They would put me out of business! I had best be moving on. Seems like everyone in Johnsbury wants ice today.

Lori: Johnsbury? Did you hear that? We're still in Johnsbury!

Mr. Morris: And there's no better place to be on July 4th, 1875—or any other time!

Jack: Did you say 1875?

Mr. Morris: Of course I did. Don't you know what year it is, young man? Where do you go to school, anyway?

Jack: Why, I go to school right here in Johnsbury. I'm in the fourth grade at the Thomas Alva Edison Middle School on Blacksmith Road.

Mr. Morris: I never heard of it. The only thing on Blacksmith Road is the blacksmith's shop.

Lori: Did you hear that? Jack, you know the old iron hitching posts in front of the video store on Blacksmith Road? They must have been the ones that the blacksmith's customers used.

Mr. Morris: Well, good-bye, all. I'll see you at the fireworks display tonight.

George: Jay-Jay! You will not believe what I just found out!

Millie: Slow down, George. Catch your breath!

George: I just heard the news down at Wilkins and Sons Confectionery Shop, and I ran all the way here without stopping.

Jay-Jay: That has to be some news, George! What is it?

George: The bone shakers are coming! They'll be here any minute.

Jack: Bone shakers? Uh-oh! Let's get out of here!

Jay-Jay: No, no, stay and watch. It's fun.

Lori: It is? Who are they, some new rock group?

George: Did you say rock group? Oh, no. You don't rock them. You ride them. Mama! Papa! Come on out quick! The bone shakers are coming!

Mama: Here we are!

Papa: Are they in sight yet?

George: I can just make them out. There must be at least ten of them.

Lori: Oh, Jack, it's a bicycle club!

Jack: Wow! It must be hard to ride those bikes. The front wheel is so big, and the back wheel is so tiny.

Bibi: Why are they called bone shakers, Jay-Jay?

Jay-Jay: Do you see how the rider's seat is right over the big front wheel? Well, riding up there makes for a very bumpy ride, especially since those wheels are made of iron. They seem to shake every bone in your body. And that's how those bicycles got to be called bone shakers.

Bibi: That's funny! Whew, there's so much dust I can hardly see.

Papa: You are certainly right about that dust, young lady. And that's just why some of us here in town think that Main Street should be paved.

Lori: Paved with what?

Papa: Why, with cobblestones, of course.

Mama: Now, now, dear, you know some of us think the town needs a library much more than cobblestones.

Papa: The library can wait.

Mama: Nonsense! . . . Let's discuss it later, shall we? You young people go into the house now and have some nice cold lemonade. It will clear the dust out of your throats.

Bibi: Thank you. That would be great.

Mama: Get some ice chips, Millie. Here is the ice pick. Mind how you use it. And George, I will be needing some more coal for the stove. There is still lots more cooking to be done for the picnic.

George: Yes, Mama.

Mama: Jay-Jay, please pump up some water and set it on the stove to boil. Your friend here can help you. Be sure there's enough water to fill all the bedroom pitchers. We will want to wash all this dust off.

Jay-Jay: Come on, Jack. I'll show you where the pump is.

Lori: Gosh, Bibi, did you hear all that? Sounds like a lot of work just to be able to wash your face and hands.

Bibi: It makes you realize how lucky we are. Just a turn of the faucet and we get all the hot and cold water we want!

Mama: What's that you girls are saying?

Lori: Uh . . . just that this is a beautiful kitchen, Ma'am. I saw a picture of one something like it in a museum . . . uh . . . I mean in a book.

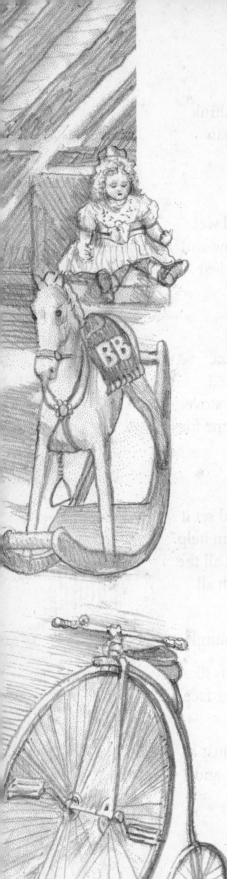

Papa: No doubt it was the latest American Kitchens Catalog you saw it in. This is a brand new type of sink, right out of the catalog. Isn't it a beauty?

Millie: It's made of iron. If you forget to dry it out after you use it, it gets rusty.

Papa: That will do, Millie. As I was saying, this is the latest in stoves. It burns coal as well as wood. And it has a perfect baking oven. Isn't that right, dear?

Mama: Yes, indeed.

Papa: There certainly are a great many new inventions nowadays. And this kitchen is right up to the minute!

Mama: I half expect that one of these days I'll go to sleep and wake up to find that some new invention has washed all the dishes and scrubbed and dried all the clothes!

Lori: I wouldn't be a bit surprised, Ma'am.

Mayor: Excuse me, folks, I knocked, but I guess you didn't hear me.

Papa: Sorry, Mr. Mayor. Come in, come on in. Won't you sit down?

Mayor: Don't mind if I do. I'm exhausted! I've been out all morning telling people about today's festivities.

Bibi: Excuse me, sir. Why didn't you just call them on the telephone?

Mayor: The tell-a-what?

Bibi: The telephone.

Mayor: I never heard of any such thing. Well, we'll be gathering on the village green in just a few minutes. Then tonight we will be shooting off fireworks in the big meadow on Duck Pond Road.

Lori: Did you hear that, Bibi? My piano teacher lives on Duck Pond Road right across the street from Livingston Mall.

Papa: You must be mistaken, young lady. I know everyone in town. There is no one here by the name of Livingston Mall. And there is no one living out on Duck Pond Road, either—except the ducks, of course.

Mama: But it is the main road leading in and out of town. And there are some of us who would be happy to see a public library built right where Duck Pond Road crosses Main Street.

Mayor: Ahem . . . well . . . uh, I think we had better get going. You are welcome to ride with me. My horse and carriage are right in front. The young people won't mind walking, I'm sure.

Papa: Thank you, Mr. Mayor. Come along, everybody. Let's not delay.

Mayor: Greetings, every . . . no, no. . . . Good afternoon, distinguished citizens of . . . no, no, no. . . . Welcome all to . . .

Mama: What are you saying, Mr. Mayor?

Mayor: Nothing, nothing. I was just thinking about my speech.

Papa: Well, I hope you've got it ready because here we are, at the village green!

All: Hooray! Hooray!

Townsperson 1: Three cheers for the mayor!

Townsperson 2: I hope the speeches aren't too long!

Mayor: Good afternoon to all you good people of Johnsbury on this glorious Fourth of July! Ninety-nine years ago, these United States became free and independent. Today we are still growing, with thirty-seven states in the Union! And I am proud to say that Johnsbury is growing right along with the rest of America.

All: Hip, hip, hooray!

Mayor: In the past few years, we have witnessed the opening of a shoe factory and a beautiful emporium filled with merchandise from far and wide. Our town newspaper is now published every week! Not only that, it has grown from a single sheet to four full pages. Furthermore, I predict that in the next year, we will see gaslights on Main Street!

All: Hooray, hooray!

Mr. Morris: But when are we going to pave Main Street? My bones can't take that rocky road anymore. Neither can my wagon. Even my horse is complaining!

Townsperson 3: Hear, hear! Main Street is the main shopping street in town. But when it rains, we ought to call it Knee-Deep-in-Mud Street! It's bad for business!

Mama: Many of us feel that it is more important for Johnsbury to build a public library. If we want our children to be ready to take their places as good citizens, they must be well informed. And for that, they must have books to read!

Townsperson 4: With all due respect, Ma'am, we have got to pave Main Street before we build a public library. Cobblestones are what we need here in Johnsbury, not more books.

Mayor: Well, maybe this is not the time to . . .

Townsperson 1: Listen here, Hillsdale isn't even as big as Johnsbury, and they have already broken ground for their public library. Do we want to be behind Hillsdale?

Jay-Jay: And do we want to ride fifteen miles to Hillsdale every time we want a book to read?

All: I should say not! No, indeed!

Papa: But the fact remains that the town does not have the money to build a library, buy books, and pave Main Street. We have to choose.

Townsperson 2: Well, speaking of money, not everyone can afford to buy books all the time. But with a public library, we could all afford to read!

Millie: That's right! I could borrow Louisa May Alcott's new book—it's called *Eight Cousins*. I would not have to save and save until I had enough money to buy it.

Lori: Oh, Millie, did you read *Little Women*? Didn't you just love it! Especially the part when . . .

Mayor: Children, children, please! Quiet!

Mr. Morris: Mr. Mayor, Mr. Mayor! Hold everything! Mr. Jackson down at the telegraph office just

received this telegram for you. He says it's urgent. Here it is, sir.

Mayor: Excuse me just a minute, good people. Let's see what this says. . . . Oh, my . . .

Townsperson 4: What does it say, Mr. Mayor? Read it out loud.

Mayor: It's from Judge Jenkins's lawyer. You remember Judge Jenkins? He passed away about a month ago. Well, his lawyer says that, according to his will, the judge left his entire collection of about two thousand books to the town of Johnsbury.

All: Oh-h-h-h!

George: Isn't that wonderful!

Townsperson 3: Two thousand books!

Mayor: It says here that Mr. Jenkins left the books to the town in gratitude for the fine education he received in the Johnsbury schools. He said the teachers were so good that he learned to read and write even though he could attend school only a few months every year.

Mama: That's right. He had to help with the planting and harvesting on his family's farm. But he went on to become a judge!

Mr. Morris: Well, I guess that settles it. We ought to build a library to hold all the books Judge Jenkins left us.

George: We'll name it Jenkins Library!

Townsperson 4: And the money we save from not having to buy books can be used to pave Main Street!

All: Yay! Hooray!

Mayor: That sounds like a good plan. We will vote on it at the next town meeting. What a Fourth of July this is turning out to be!

Jay-Jay: And just wait until the Fourth of July next year. I just heard that President Ulysses S. Grant issued a proclamation only yesterday. He said that a Centennial Exhibition will be held in Philadelphia in 1876 to celebrate the one-hundredth birthday of the United States of America. Won't that be grand?

Mayor: Three cheers for Old Glory!

All: Hip, hip, hooray!

Mayor: That's all for now, people of Johnsbury. I hope to see everyone at the fireworks display tonight.

Mama: Millie, George, Jay-Jay, please gather up your things. It's time to get back to the house.

Mr. Morris: Excuse me, Ma'am, would you mind if I drop in later on? My niece is visiting. She is studying to be a librarian, and given your interest in the library and all, I thought you might like to meet her. There she is talking to the mayor. Her name is Barbara Blake.

Mama: We would be delighted to meet your niece. Jay-Jay, why don't you go over to Miss Blake and present her with our compliments.

Jay-Jay: All right, Mother. I'll be home in a few minutes. I want to take that family picture before it gets dark.

Papa: Good. I will get everyone posed for you.

Jack: Oh, boy, what a day!

Lori: It has been great! But have you two thought about how we're going to get back home to our own Fourth of July celebration?

Bibi: Maybe we should talk to Jay-Jay about that.

Jack: Here he comes now. You know, Jay-Jay, it's been a great day, but we've got to be getting home.

Jay-Jay: I know. Don't worry, I can help you. I'll just take the family picture first, since everyone is in place.

Jack: Why don't you let me take it, Jay-Jay. I'm a good photographer—really!

Millie: Do let him, Jay-Jay. It will be the first time you've ever been in a family picture.

Jay-Jay: All right. Lori, Bibi, why don't you take a look under the hood, too?

Jack: Yes, come see, Lori!

Bibi: Move over, you two. Make room for me under there!

Jack: Hey, do you feel as if we're moving?

Bibi: Yes, we're going into the picture!

Lori: Hang on! Here we go again!

Bibi, Lori, and Jack: Good-bye, Jay-Jay! 'Bye, everyone!

Jack: We're back in Grammy's attic!

Bibi: And look—here's Jay-Jay's camera. There's a picture on it.

Lori: No, there are two pictures. Look, this is the picture that Jack took. See? Jay-Jay's in it.

Bibi: And this one is a wedding picture. Oh, my goodness, Jay-Jay is the groom!

Jack: What does it say on the back? The writing is so faded.

Lori: It says, "The wedding of . . . Barbara . . . Blake and Jack . . . Jessup, June 10, 1876."

Bibi: Jack Jessup—that's your name, too, Jack! Jay-Jay must have been his nickname! "J. J." Get it?

Jack: I guess I was named after him. I never knew that. You know, he must have been our great-great-grandfather.

Bibi: And Barbara Blake is "B.B." This is her rocking horse. That means she was our great-great-grandmother!

Jack: Oh, boy! Jay-Jay was right. We were right in the middle of our history.

Bibi: I'm sure there's a lot more family history that Grammy can tell us about.

Lori: There's a lot more Johnsbury history that we can find out about, too. Let's go down to the library tomorrow and look in the town records.

Bibi: You know what? This Fourth of July has turned out to be the greatest!

Bibi, Lori, and Jack: Hip, hip, hooray!

Little Talk

by Aileen Fisher

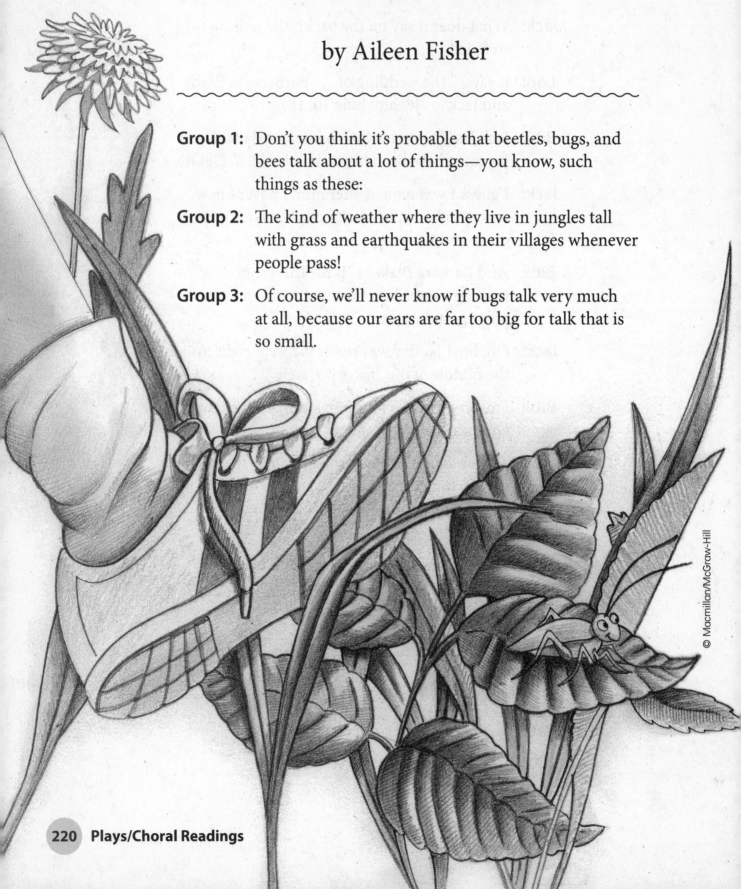

Group 1: Don't you think it's probable that beetles, bugs, and bees talk about a lot of things—you know, such things as these:

Group 2: The kind of weather where they live in jungles tall with grass and earthquakes in their villages whenever people pass!

Group 3: Of course, we'll never know if bugs talk very much at all, because our ears are far too big for talk that is so small.

But I Wonder....

by Aileen Fisher

Solo 1: The crickets in the thickets,

Solo 2: and the katydids in trees,

Solo 3: and ants on plants, and butterflies,

Solo 4: and ladybugs and bees

Group 1: don't smell with little noses but with feelers,
if you please.

Group 2: They get along quite nicely,
but I wonder how they sneeze.

© Macmillan/McGraw-Hill

Think-Aloud
COPYING MASTERS

I wonder . . .

I made a
connection when . . .

Think-Aloud Copying Master 3

I figured out _____ because . . .

Think-Aloud Copying Master 4

227

I thought _____ was important in this text because . . .

When I read _____,
I had to re-read,
read back, read on . . .

LITERATURE INDEX by GENRE

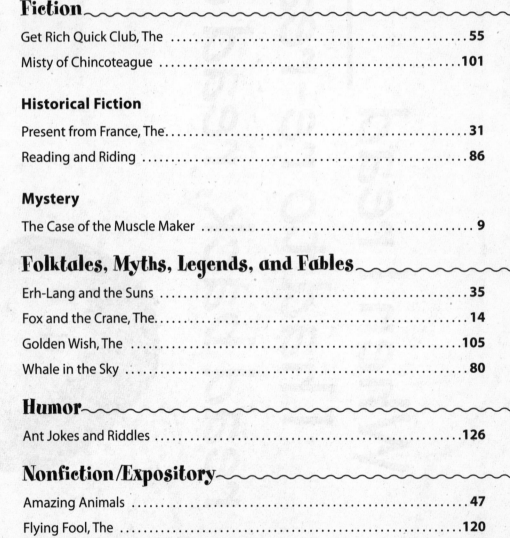

ACKNOWLEDGMENTS ~~~~~~~~~~~~~~~~~~~~~~~ Continued

"Long Trip" from THE COLLECTED POEMS OF LANGSTON HUGHES by Langston Hughes. Copyright © 1994 by The Estate of Langston Hughes. Used by permission of Alfred A. Knopf, a division of Random House, Inc.

"Reading and Riding" from *Storyworks*, September 2002, Vol. 10, Issue 1. Copyright © 2002 by Scholastic Inc. Used by permission of Scholastic Inc.

"ANOTHER OP'NIN', ANOTHER SHOW" Words and Music by COLE PORTER. Copyright © 1949 (Renewed) CHAPPELL & CO. Reprinted by permission of ALFRED PUBLISHING CO., INC. All Rights Reserved.

"On Our Own" from KON-TIKI: A TRUE ADVENTURE OF SURVIVAL AT SEA by Thor Heyerdahl, adapted by Lisa Norby. Copyright © 1984 by Random House, Inc. Used by permission of Random House, Inc.

"Small Artist Has a Big Appeal" by Fabiola Santiago from *The Miami Herald*, Thursday, June 5, 2003. Copyright © 2003 by The Miami Herald. Used by permission.

Excerpt from MISTY OF CHINCOTEAGUE by Marguerite Henry. Copyright © 1947, renewed 1975 by Marguerite Henry. Used by permission of Macmillan Publishing Company.

"The Golden Wish" from THE GOLDEN HOARD: MYTHS AND LEGENDS OF THE WORLD by Geraldine McCaughrean. Copyright © 1995 by Geraldine McCaughrean. Used by permission of Margaret K. McElderry Books, an imprint of Simon & Schuster Children's Publishing Division.

"Darkness Is My Friend" from MOUSE TAIL MOON by Joanne Ryder. Copyright © 2002 by Joanne Ryder. Used by permission of Henry Holt and Company, LLC.

MARY ANNING AND THE SEA DRAGON by Jeannine Atkins. Copyright © 1999 by Jeannine Atkins. Used by permission of Douglas & McIntyre Ltd.

"The Flying Fool" by Thomas Fleming from *Boys' Life*, Vol. 94, Issue 5 (2004). Copyright © 2004 by Boys' Life. Used by permission of Boy Scouts of America.

Cover Illustration: Robert Van Nutt

Illustration Credits: Amanda Harvey, 9–13; Robert Van Nutt, 14–16; Renee Daily, 17–19; Dan Krovatin, 20–23; Eva Cockrille, 24–27; Gil Ashby, 28–30; Gioia Fiammenghi, 31–34; Chi Chung, 35–39, 153–166; Timothy Otis, 40–43, 86–89; Gerry O'Neill, 44–46; Donald Cook, 47–50; Gershom Griffith, 51–54; Paige Billin-Frye, 55–58; Barbara Pollack, 59–61, 132–152; Erin Eitter Kono, 66–71, 90–92; Joel Iskowitz, 72–76, 203–219; Paula Wendland, 80–82; Kelly Murphy, 83–85; Laurie Harden, 93–96; Jan Naimo Jones, 97–100; Susan Spellman, 101–104; Valerie Sokolova, 105–110; Janet Hamlin, 111–113; David Erickson, 114–119; Roman Dunets, 120–125; Terri Murphy, 126–129; Betsy James, 167–181; Fian Arroyo, 182–202; Kate Flanagan, 220–221